My Years of M[o]
Sex and Drugs [in the Florida]
Pill Mill

by Christian Valdes

With Joel & Lisa Canfield

The Author on the job.

Table of Contents

Part 3: Chris

Introduction

For 5 years, I was at the center of the biggest drug operation in America.

It was an operation that became internationally notorious, insanely violent and nonstop freaky. It made its kingpins millions and millions of dollars, and it made me as much money as there were hours in the day -- because there were endless numbers of people lining up for what I had the power to give them. And, by the way, those people were willing to do just about anything to get it. With the men, that generally meant money. With the women, that meant money - *and* almost any kind of sexual arrangement I was after.

But here's the fun part about this operation – it was *completely legal.*

Yeah, that's right. It did its business out in broad daylight, mostly in the same kinds of strip malls where you might get a Subway sandwich or drop off your dry-cleaning. Of course, there were all sorts of transactions going on *inside* this operation that weren't legal – but nobody was really paying attention.

Well, back that up. *I* was paying attention – because I was the mastermind behind a lot of those transactions.

From 2004 to 2009, I rode this money train for all it was worth -- until suddenly it wasn't worth much anymore. Not only that, I walked away free and clear; the only time I got busted was in the head by the nightsticks of a couple of dirty cops who wanted to scare the shit out of me. Others weren't so lucky – including the victim of one horrible personal tragedy that helped scare me straight. But up until then, it was a 24/7 party fueled by easy money. A party that seemed like it had no end in sight.

So what exactly was this drug operation all about?

Well, it didn't involve the usual suspects - cocaine, meth, pot or heroin. No, the kind of drugs I'm talking about were *legally prescribed by genuine doctors*. Sure, they were legit - but that didn't make them any less lethal. Actually, it made them *more* lethal. Back in the time period I'm talking about, prescription drugs were killing *five times* as many people as illegal drugs, according to the Medical Examiners Association. And the pills *our* doctors were making available became the deadliest, just because they were way-too-easy to get.

I didn't see that part of the equation at the time. To me, everyone involved was an adult and knew what they were getting into.

"Pill mills." That's what the media called the pain clinics I managed. We gave out heavy-hitter drugs like Xanax, Percocet, Oxycontin, Roxicodone and Methadone just like they were candy. And because Florida didn't have any systems in place to keep track of any prescriptions, somebody could easily go into one clinic and get some Oxy and then head over to a different clinic for some more a few minutes later. I know how easy it was – because I helped a whole lot of people do just that (including my posse of stripper pals – but more on them later).

That's because I was running my own operation *within* the operation.

I started my own thing as the whole pain clinic set-up spiraled out of control. With so much profit to be made, a lot of pain clinics suddenly morphed into genuine drug dealers, shoving as many patients through the doctors' doors as humanly possible to make as much cash as they could. To stay competitive or even just to be able to stay in business, other pain clinics had to follow suit. The money was irresistible; clinic owners and doctors were buying yachts and Lamborghinis with *cash*. The abuse was unbelievable; typically, a patient with genuine pain issues might get 30 or so pain pills prescribed per month – but, at the height of the Florida pain pill insanity, suddenly those prescriptions would be written for *300 or 500* pills a month. Not only that, but a patient might get a couple scrips, maybe one for Oxys, one for Percs - meaning they could end up with *800 to 1000 pills* from just one visit

Best case scenario, that kind of dosage would turn the patients into hopeless junkies if they actually took them all. The worst case? Well, let's just say they wouldn't show up for their next pain clinic appointments – or any other appointments anywhere else.

And let's be clear, at that point, most of those "patients" weren't really patients any longer. They were hustlers, plain and simple. They faked drug tests and MRIs to get the pills they wanted, because they were either addicts or dealers or a combination of the two. And they might have come a thousand miles or more to get what they were after.

During this time, the I-75, the main highway north out of Florida into Georgia, Tennessee, and Kentucky and right up into Canada, became known as the "Oxy Express." Dealers would drive down the Interstate into South Florida, pick up hundreds or even thousands of pills at a whole bunch of pain clinics, and drive right back home and sell those pills for about 100 times the going price in the Sunshine State.

Make no mistake about it, Florida was ground zero for pain pill abuse. In 2010, CNN called South Florida the pain clinic capital of America and the mass media did story after story on the nightmare. At one point, the country's top 50 prescription pain pill sellers were in Florida – and 33 of those 50 were in Broward County, where I got involved in the racket. There were more than 150 storefront pain clinics in Broward at the height of the madness.

The part of it that's really fucked up? Florida *knew* this was a huge problem. In 2004, the year I first got into the game, assistant statewide prosecutor Oscar Gelpi called Florida's prescription drug free-for-all a public safety problem and said the state's lack of action was "dangerous and irresponsible." But it took five more years for the lawmakers to pass a bill to set up a statewide prescription database, designed to finally stop the pill pushers in their tracks.

In 2011, though, new governor Rick Scott took office and shut down the money to pay for the database. His background? Well, he was the CEO of a string of health care facilities and oversaw what the Miami Herald called "the largest Medicare fraud in the nation's history." So that's where he was coming from – that kind of mentality was now in charge of the whole state. But the backlash was immediate and effective – officials were so desperate to stop this shit that they raised the money for the database in the private sector. In any event, the pill party was finally over.

The funny part of it all was that when I got involved in all this monkey business, I thought I was getting *out* of the drug racket. I was already a successful weed grower and seller who was looking for a legitimate career – and I thought I found it in pain management. But when I realized what was really going on – and when I saw how I was treated by the "management" - I went after my own piece of the pie, as well as a lot of other treats on the side.

This is a story that could only happen in South Florida. Just like I'm a guy you would only find in South Florida.

My name is Christian Valdes – and by the way, that's one of the last actual names you're going to read in this book, because I had to change a lot of them to tell my story (some events have also been moved around for legal reasons). You'll find out everything about me later, but, for now, here's the short version.

I'm a full-blooded Cuban who was born right here in the U.S. I'm also the kind of guy who, if you saw me walking down the street, you might actually cross to the other side, because, to be honest, my appearance kind of scares the shit out of some people. My upper torso is covered with tattoos, my arms are bulging with muscles and I got a diamond grill over the bottom teeth of my mouth. Since I have a concealed weapons permit, sometimes I'm also packing a pistol.

So yeah, if you're an out-of-towner, you might worry about what I'm gonna do to you if I'm walking towards you. Well, what I'm gonna do is nothing. I don't hassle innocent people, I don't pick fights and I don't look for trouble. But if you cross me or do wrong by me, look out - because I don't walk away from a confrontation either. On the contrary – I embrace it.

Here's a story that will give you an idea of who I am and what I'm all about. It'll also explain why, even though I saw millions of pain pills exchange hands when I was in the clinic business, I never took one of them myself.

I was 18 or 19 and I had gotten myself thrown out of high school – I ended up finishing up through an online course. You'll get the details on that later. Anyway, I was still living with my mom and stepdad, who had a place in a nice gated community in Pembroke Pines, north of Miami, south of Fort Lauderdale. I was running with a crew that was dealing weed and I was making okay money from that. While I was doing that, I naturally met other people selling other things. One of them tells me he has these new pills, they were called Xanax.

Xanax? Hadn't heard about that one, but hey, any pill with a name that started with an X and ended with an X had to be interesting, so why not try it out? I buy like 60 of them.

Friday night rolls around – and I had just sold about a half pound of weed for one of my friends. Because I unloaded it so fast, I'm done early – it's only around 9 and I'm loaded with cash from all my transactions, hanging out with this guy who supplied the weed and two other guys. I figure, let's make something happen with the rest of the night - what the hell, I'll try two bars of Xanax, which is around 4 milligrams, and wash 'em down with a lot of alcohol to see what happens. So I do just that.

Next thing, it's Sunday morning. I lost a day and a half.

I had blacked out and woke up in my bed at home with a foggy head and a lot of questions. Like, who the fuck took me home and put me in my bed? Also, where the fuck are my keys, my wallet and all the stuff in my pockets?

I look around my room and finally spot my stuff. I reach for my wallet first because I knew I had about $400, maybe $500 in it from selling the weed Friday night and wanted to make sure it was okay. I open it up...and there's only 30 bucks in it.

Well, that's funny.

I go eat breakfast to clear my head, so I can figure out what the hell happened. I try and try to remember, but nothing comes back. And then I get a call – it's the guy that gave me the weed to sell. Let's call him Asshole #1.

He's being friendly at first. He's like, "All right, I'm going to come by and get my money for the weed you got rid of for me. I said, "Hey, I woke up here and I don't have anything on me. I was with you all. You tell me what the fuck happened Friday after I blacked out. What the fuck happened?"

He can't or, more accurately, won't answer my question.

He deflects. He says I was belligerent, I was fighting with the three of them and some other people. And he says he has no idea where my money went. He's lying.

I can tell by the way he's talking, he and the other two guys robbed me. They were who I was hanging with and they were obviously the ones who took me home, put me into bed and emptied my wallet.

Only he's acting like I owe *him* money.

Let me again be clear – I'm a stand-up guy. As long as you're good to me, as long as you're straight with me, I'll do anything for you. You can rely on me to treat you with respect and honesty. Again, I don't get into fights over nothing – but I also don't walk away from a conflict.

Anyway, our conversation is escalating and escalating. Threats are being made. I keep cool and I finally say to Asshole #1, "Look, buddy, I'm not going to pay you the money you think you're going to get. I know you guys already got it – and more. You think you're being slick, but it's obvious what you're trying to pull."

His answer? "Well, I think I'm gonna come over and collect by doing $300 worth of damage to your face."

"Okay," I say. "I'll let you right in. Come on in. You think you're bad? Come on through."

End of conversation.

I go down to get ready. On my way, I tell my mom, "If these three kids show up at the gate, tell the guard to let them in. "She's a little alarmed, because she can tell something's going down.

It's the middle of the day on Sunday. It's a time when gated communities are usually pretty quiet, maybe a couple of kids playing outside, some people doing some yard work, that kind of thing. A little enclosed suburbia. And here I come, walking down the street, wearing only shorts and sneakers - and carrying a little something extra. My stepdad's aluminum softball bat.

My mom's house is near the back of the gated community. I march straight towards the front, where the gate is, where they have to come through. I stop when I see them driving through the middle of the complex – they don't see me, and they head for the cul-de-sac where I live. And incidentally, it's also where a friend of mine, Nacho, lives. He's in his backyard, looking at me and knowing something's up. But he's on house arrest, so he can't go far or his ankle bracelet will signal the cops.

The car comes down to the cul-de-sac where I'm standing solo, bat in hand. All three of the guys from Friday night are in the car, including Asshole #1, the one who threatened me on the phone - he's in the back seat of the car with the window down. I go up to that open window. I stick the bat out so it's in his face and I poke at it.

"Get out of the fucking car," I say. "You want to threaten me, bitch? Then get out."

He's scared. He ain't moving. But the driver, who we'll call Asshole #2, gets out of the car and starts talking to me, he's just a couple of feet away from me.

I don't care about Asshole #2. My anger is burning and it's all directed at Asshole #1, the guy in the backseat who was punking me on the phone. I honestly want to kill him.

Asshole #2, though, keeps coming at me. "Why don't you put down the bat and fight like a man?"

Okay. Wish granted.

I drop the bat and BAM. I start unloading on this kid. I'm on top of him drilling his face with my fists as bad as I could. You might say I'm a little preoccupied, so guess what happens? Asshole #1 decides to finally come out, because he thinks he can take me down while I'm busy with Asshole #2. So he dropkicks me in the head and knocks me off.

So now I got both of them on me, the third guy doesn't even want to come out of the car. They pick me up. They throw me on top of the car. They pull me down and slam me around some more. It's two on one and I'm in trouble. They slam me into the car one more time and I slide off the side, out of their reach. Out of the corner of my eye, I see the bat – right there on the ground, calling for me. I run for it.

Asshole #2, the driver that first came at me? I know it's his car, it's brand new and he's only had it a week. He comes after me to block me from the bat – which could fuck up that new car badly. But I get the bat before he gets to me – and I bash in the back windshield with it, just so he knows what fucking time it is.

So he's really pissed – but I've still got the bat. "You want to come hit me?" I say. He puts his arm up to protect himself. No problem. I take a swing at the arm. I shatter his elbow and break his arm. He falls to the ground in pain. Now Asshole #3, the third guy in this trio, he just takes off, he knows suddenly the tables are turned and he doesn't want any part of it.

But Asshole #1, the one who made it so I wanted to take some batting practice? He runs the other way and ends up dead-ended at Nacho's house. Nacho's got my back, so Asshole #1 has no choice but to turn and face me.

We're facing each other in almost the same fighting stance – but he thinks he's fast enough to get away from me. He's not. He tries to do a spin move, but I clobber him on the shoulder with the bat as he's flying around – he goes down hard on the concrete. He gets back up and runs over to the car.

Where the cops have arrived.

There's a swarm of them, they got their guns out and those guns are trained on me. Asshole #2 is still on the ground, screaming in pain and, me, I'm a bloody mess myself, my knuckles, my arms, my hands, all covered with the red stuff. I get down on the ground and so does Asshole #1.

What happens next? Well, nothing. None of us were about to press charges, so none of us got arrested. The cops had no choice but to let us go. We all just beat the shit out of each other, gave the development a little Sunday afternoon entertainment, and everybody got to go home scot-free.

But I was lucky. Incidents like that were why I didn't stray much from pot. Later on, I'd have a much bigger reason never to try the pills that were flying around right and left at the clinics I managed. Mainly...I saw what those pills did to our clientele. It wasn't pretty. But you're about to find out all that out for yourself.

Hope you enjoy the read.

Christian Valdes, February, 2015

PART 1

NINO BREEZY

Chapter 1: Beginnings

I was born in 1979 in North Miami Beach, Florida. My parents had emigrated legally to the U.S. from Cuba a few years earlier, starting their new life in America in the Garden State, New Jersey. Jersey, however, didn't meet my dad's expectations, so, when a couple of friends in Miami told him he should move South and take advantage of some business opportunities, he jumped at the chance.

My dad was a mechanic, so he started out by working at few local car shops. But he wasn't the type of guy who was going to spend his whole life working for other people, so he always had an eye on the next step. That's a mindset he taught me. Back then, he only needed a down payment of 10K to get his own gas and repair place, so he got it together and bought a gas station on 79th Street, right down from the Kennedy

Causeway near Miami Shores. It was a good investment - he sold it about 15 years later for about a million dollars.

I grew up speaking Spanish at home and learning English at school. As a kid, I liked watching fighting and boxing, and I also loved the normal boy stuff like He-Man and the Masters of the Universe, GI Joe, the Marvel superheroes...as a matter of fact, I still own a few action figures from that time. And, as you'll see, every once in a while, I turned into an action figure myself

My dad was tough and so was my older brother. Like me, neither of them were bullies – they just looked out for themselves and for their own. My dad, he'd go out to his gas station at around 5 in the morning every day intent on taking care of business. And he did, even in a neighborhood that wasn't the best. Sometimes he'd catch guys trying to steal gas from him. Or maybe they'd try to short him what he was owed on fixing a car. Whatever, he wasn't having it. Sometimes he'd physically fight them and sometimes he'd even pull out his gun in broad daylight and shoot at them as they were trying to drive away – I remember hearing gunshots from inside of the gas station. He was a nice man, but he wasn't gonna let you screw with him or his business. If you got on his bad side, he was going to strike back fast, you wouldn't even see it coming. I saw that and also took that attitude on board.

As for my brother, he looked out for me. One time in elementary school, some kid picked on me and had me crying. I didn't know how to fight at that time and my brother didn't really know how to either – but later, the things he did to this kid, beating the shit out of him for what he did to me? Wow. I really looked up to him after that.

So, yeah, I saw that to settle a score, you had to do what you had to do. It was how you kept respect and how you held on to what was yours.

When I was around 6 or 7, my parents split up. The divorce motivated my mom to get a career of her own – so she went to the Police Academy in Broward County, north of Miami, and there, she met the man who was to become my stepdad, who also in law enforcement. When she graduated from the

Academy, she also got a job with in law enforcement – so she moved up there and I went with her. My brother stayed with my dad down in Miami-Dade. I was too young to know why we got split up the way we did, but, as my brother was older, I can only think that he was able to do more with my dad at the time and maybe they figured I still needed my mom for a few more years. Who knows?

But I got along great with my stepdad. We fished, we played basketball, racquetball and tennis and we golfed a couple of times. We did everything together. At school, I was a pretty good student too. No trouble.

Then came high school. Then came lots of trouble.

Chapter 2: High School High

After I finished middle school, my mom and stepdad had enough money to make the move into a nice gated community in Pembroke Pines – and right from the get-go, I started running with the wrong crowd at my new high school, Cooper City High. I got into drug-dealing - and believe it or not, it kind of happened because of my work ethic.

I'm the type of person who has always had a job – a real job – since I was 15 years old. I *work*. But that only gets you so far these days. My first job, I was making $6 an hour at McDonalds. That didn't cut it. The fact is, then and now, jobs don't give you enough to live on. Everybody I know has to have something going on the side to have enough to pay the bills as well as put clothes on your back and food on the table. That's America now.

Like I said, I learned from my dad the importance of building your own business and being in control of it, so you're not under somebody else's thumb - you never know when that thumb might decide to squash you. The way he was raised in Cuba, you do for yourself. That's why he left - you might have to work back there for about ten cents a week, and he couldn't see a decent future based on that kind of bullshit.

So I wanted to do for myself too. My mom wasn't giving me any money, maybe a five or a ten every now and then for a haircut or a meal, but I wanted my own income stream, so I could do what I wanted when I wanted. From ninth grade on, I started dealing weed. Little nickel and dime bags. I sold a little cocaine, some acid, but mostly pot. Something to keep a little money in my hands and keep me eating. To take a girl out if I wanted to. Whatever. I wanted freedom and I wanted options.

My mom knew something was going on. There were too many times where she'd have to tell the guards at the gate to let in people she didn't know, people that I'd tell my mom I was going to play basketball with or meeting at the development's pool. Then there were the weird phone calls that would come in for me from *more* people she didn't recognize and she'd wonder what *those* were all about. I mean, was I making ten new friends a week or something? Eventually, she caught on that I was doing something on the side besides making burgers and fries at Mickey D's, and she stopped giving me those fives and tens. And I, of course, stop asking for them because I didn't really need them.

But she still couldn't admit to herself I was doing anything wrong.

You know how mothers are with their kids, they turn a blind eye to a lot of stuff that they don't want to see. Plus you have to remember that both her and my stepfather were *cops.* He suspected more than she did, but she continued to defend me. And I did my best to keep what I was doing far away from the house.

But the money was too good to pass up – there were always buyers anxious to get what they wanted. I mean, it wasn't like I was selling magazine subscriptions or something - nobody's calling you up at midnight desperate to get a copy of *People* or *Sports Illustrated*. No, weed was easy to sell because everyone was after it. It seemed like almost everyone I knew was a pothead. Including me.

For me, weed was the safe drug. To this day, I'd rather smoke weed than anything else. It relaxes me and I like things that relax me – for example, coke, that made me crazy. As a matter of fact, pretty much everything else seemed too dangerous, especially after my experience with Xanax. Later on, when I was swimming in pain pills, this attitude would definitely save my life.

So, yeah, weed was a friend – and, because of it, I met someone else who would become a really good friend. As a matter of fact, he became my best buddy during high school.

It started with a girl who went to the same high school as me. She lived in the same gated community and I sold her weed.

Turned out her dad, who was our mailman, was also a complete stoner. I ended up dealing to him too. And then her dad hooked me up with a couple of his friends that would buy from me. All in all, a good neighbor to have.

But these people were more than neighbors. They were kind of my surrogate family. The dad was real nice and was always looking after us. He would rather have us in his house smoking pot instead of going out on the streets and doing something stupid that would get us in trouble. A different parenting approach, but maybe he was right to think that way.

That's how I met J Nasty, the girl's little brother. He was four years younger than me, but it didn't matter. We started hanging and he became like *my* brother. We would party together, we would get into fights together and we would sell together. J Nasty was a Gemini just like me, our birthdays were right around the corner from each other, and it felt like we were torn from the same cloth. We had that kind of connection.

But no matter how hard J Nasty's folks tried to keep me indoors, I was still running around plenty. Me and a few other guys formed our own gang, we called it the Smoking Blunts Crew. And we got in a bunch of trouble. My mom was always getting calls from the school and she and my stepdad were having trouble dealing with what was going on. Besides being worried about me, since they were also cops, this was potentially a very embarrassing situation for them.

Finally, they figured they had to do something – so they called up my dad back down in North Miami. Result? I had to go live with my Papi and go to high school down there. I guess they figured he could handle me better than them, plus I'd get away from the "bad company" I had surrounded myself with.

Well, that arrangement only lasted five or six months. I didn't know anybody in Miami and I wanted out. Plus a new high school was opening back in my old neighborhood, Flanagan High School. My old friends said they were going to start there in the fall – and I should be there too. I told my dad I didn't want to live with him anymore. Our relationship wasn't great at the time. I felt Papi hadn't been there a lot of the time for me after he and my mom split up. Anyway, me moving back made the relationship even worse. It would be a few years before we saw each other again.

Thankfully, my mom took me back. She always had a special place in her heart for me and would never turn me away. Maybe that heart was too big, because when I came back, she ended up paying a really steep price.

It may have been a brand new high school – but, when it came to me, the same old problems were in play. If anything, they got worse. More fights, more drug dealing, more gang activity. And because of my stupidity…my mom lost her job. She was always being called away from work to come rescue me. I would get caught smoking weed at school. Skipping school. In a fight. Car accidents. Even robbing somebody's house.

I was an idiot.

Anyway, her bosses got tired of her getting pulled away from her job - she had too much baggage thanks to me, and they let her go. But I wasn't done fucking up yet. What was supposed to be my senior year was suddenly turning into yet another junior year. I was going to be a couple credits shy of being able to graduate, so I would have to repeat the year.

Except I didn't. Because they threw me out of Flanagan before I ever got the chance.

Here's what went down. Me and this black kid were having a dumb conflict over a basketball game. I wanted to fight, he didn't want to. So he went to tell the teacher on me. Now, this wasn't just any teacher – this was an ex-NFL player who was a teacher/coach on staff, so he was way bigger than me and he was tough. And I think he already had a chip on his shoulder about me for whatever reason.

So I'm in the gym, with my backpack on and this teacher gets in my face. He's walking forward and deliberately physically provoking me. He's pushing me back with his body. I don't want to rumble with a teacher – I'm not *that* stupid. So I say,

"This doesn't have to be like this." But he doesn't stop. He pushes me so hard that I finally lose it. I put down the backpack and open up on him.

Well, he takes the punches and simply picks me up like *I'm* a backpack – and he throws me into the wall. He then throws me into the bleachers. He picks me back up again, I'm still trying to punch him down, and he throws me into another wall.

He's still not done and he grabs me again. I'm in the air, punching and punching at his face, trying to get him to let me go. He's still bashing me up against everything in sight. He finally pushes my head through the double doors leading out of the gym, and he takes me out to this huge open area at the school while I continue to drill him in his face. It might have been funny to watch, if you weren't the guy being introduced to every nearby wall.

Finally, he gets tired of playing with me and puts me down. I get thrown into IS, Internal Suspension, where I have to sit for the rest of the day.

But that wasn't why I got expelled. That happens *after* school.

The bell finally rings and I go out to wait for the bus. I'm talking to some girls that live in my neighborhood. I see them looking behind me, looking a little rattled. They're like, "Chris, don't turn around, there are some black guys coming up behind you."

Fucking pussy.

I knew these clowns were coming for me because of the kid I had the original beef with. He didn't want to fight me one-on-one, but now he's coming with four of his friends to take me out. He's a fucking pussy and my blood is boiling. The girls are trying to protect me from getting a beat down, but I don't care. As soon as they alert me to what's coming at me, I'm putting down my backpack for the second time that day.

I turn around. All five of them are standing there. BAM, I go after the kid and the two guys next to him. But there's two others, so they grab me and hold onto me. I can't beat the odds. But I'm sure gonna try. I break free and keep swinging.

Now teachers are getting involved, trying to break up the fight. *They* accidentally get hit a couple times and I push them out of the way. I want to finish this. But it's too big a mess. There's a crowd, there's a commotion and the fight is over.

I just walk off campus and I never come back.

In a way, it worked out. I didn't have to do another year at Flanagan. I had my transcripts sent over to an online education company and easily made up the credits I needed in a lot less time. I got my ring and I got a diploma. I'm a high school graduate. And that's good to say.

In that way, I wasn't an idiot.

Chapter 3: Growing

Author with his homegrown crop

Photo © Copyright 2014 Christian Valdes

I finished my high school education, but my buddy, J. Nasty, ended up dropping out after the ninth grade. I was pissed. I'm like, "Dude, look at me, I'm a piece of garbage, but I finished up high school. You're smart enough to go further. Don't do this."

He did it anyway. What are you gonna do? My folks couldn't do anything with me, I wasn't gonna be able to do anything with him.

I was still at home with my stepdad and my mom, who had gotten a new job in a doctor's office. I had gotten a new job too, during my last year of school at Flanagan. I was done with McDonalds and, for whatever reason, I now didn't want to work around people any more, they drove me crazy. Maybe it was a control thing again. Anyway, now my ambition was to be around animals. I liked animals, we had plenty of them at our house. I felt like an animal would never do you wrong, they're kind and friendly as long as you treat them good. That was the big difference between them and people.

So I started working at a kennel. It wasn't bad. You go in, you feed the dogs, bathe them, clean their cages and you walk them. It's an easy job and nobody's watching what you're doing every second of your shift.

This is where I have to explain something else about myself – when I work, I'm serious, I'm responsible and I show up. In other words, I'm a professional – I get the job done. All the trouble I got into at school, all the trouble I got into at clubs while I was drinking and partying? That doesn't happen when I'm working. Maybe it's my split Gemini personality, but, in the workplace, I'm a guy you can count on. I always deliver – and, at the same time, I also want to be recognized for delivering.

Remember all that – because it's all gonna come into play later.

Anyway, my successful experience working with dogs allowed me to get a job as a vet tech. That put me working with a veterinarian side-by-side and helping them during surgery. I would also prep dogs and cats for their treatments. I was really good at this, which is why it got to the point where, even though I wasn't really licensed to do it, I was able to spay and neuter dogs and cats on my own. I was a whiz at it.

That's the smart half of me. Unfortunately, the stupid half was also hard at work. After my 18th birthday, I was able to be officially arrested – so naturally I was. And naturally, it was because of another fight.

A friend of mine who had also been expelled from high school had his phone stolen by another kid who played baseball for Flanagan. I went over to his house one morning and we smoked some pot, while he went on about Joe Baseball stealing his phone. He's planning on kicking the kid's ass when he gets out of school – and he wants me to come along to back him up. This is all he wants to talk about and I finally agree to come along.

We park outside the school and walk towards the campus as the bell rings. Sure enough, here comes Joe Baseball walking out towards us as we're approaching the school. My friend confronts him. He starts talking shit to him about what we're going to do to him. He just kept on talking and talking for five or ten minutes. It was irritating me. Where I'm from, we don't talk much.

So I finally said to my buddy, "Dude – hit him like this."

And I hit Joe Baseball with a left. It looked like his eye exploded. He fell to the ground. My friend takes advantage of the fact that I took the first shot and jumps on him. As that happens, other jocks from the school surround me and start pushing me around – they're looking out for their own. But they don't want to actually fight, because more and more people are coming around and they can't get caught in the middle of a brawl.

I'm saying, "Let me go, I'm not even going to this fucking school anymore!" They did as I asked, but I couldn't help hitting Joe Baseball a couple more times to make sure he got the message not to mess with my friend anymore.

Next thing I know, the police officer from the school has me. We got arrested for the fight because we weren't students there no more. The cops knew who we were - and they weren't fooling around. They were like, "You're going to fucking jail. We're not giving you a chance. You had a chance when you walked out of here, when we expelled you. Now you're back here doing shit again."

So I went to jail for a couple of days. And when I got out, I got my first tattoo, but definitely not my last. That first one was a pair of fuzzy dice I had put on my right arm along with the words, "Mi Vida Loca." If you didn't know, that means "My Crazy Life" in Spanish.

That craziness was only getting more and more out of control.

I finally moved out of my mom and stepdad's place. And probably not for the reason you'd expect. It was because of a dog. I had gotten a huge Rottweiler Mastiff, but my mom didn't want another animal in the house. I said, "You have ten cats, I can't have a dog of my own?" She said, "No. You want to keep this dog, you have to get your own place."

I thought about it. I was over 18, I had a job, I had extra money from dealing, I had a car, a black Pontiac Bonneville...I could do it. I could get the hell out of there and get my own place.

So I did. I could afford it, because I had made a valuable new connection.

During my last year at Flanagan, another Cuban, who I'll call Juan, became a good buddy of mine. He was dating a girl from my neighborhood that I was good friends with and we took a shine to each other.

Juan was coming around with a lot of weed to sell and I didn't know where it was coming from. All I knew was he would bring in a pound and it would be in a gold coffee can with a fake coffee label on it – it all seemed very pro. He was very vague about his sources and I didn't pursue it any further. It wasn't my business, the important thing was I could get plenty to sell and at a very good price.

After about a year of buying and dealing from him, he suddenly started opening up to me. I guess he had to work with me for a while to make sure I was an okay person and that I had street credibility. I proved that I did, I sold his stuff fast and brought back his money the next day.

On top of that, if there were any problems with anybody else, I always had his back if he needed me to step up. I was more comfortable with being physical, if it was required, than he was – so I acted as the bodyguard and bouncer if need be. It was the role I would continue to play in the pain clinics. People knew that I wasn't afraid to handle a situation if it needed to be handled – and that, at the same time, I was a responsible guy who was loyal to those who took care of me.

That's what happened with Juan. Basically, I became his right-hand man and he recognized that. And he knew it was time to take me to the next level.

So he told me what was going down. I found out he had people growing the stuff in rented houses down south. Now, he wanted *me* to grow – and he started teaching me how it was done.

Those lessons began with what *not* to do – because the last thing you want to do is get busted with a house full of weed. Now, the easiest way to get caught growing is through your electric bill. Since you have to keep lights on the plants at least 12 hours a day, your power usage spikes – and the Florida Power & Light company will alert the cops.

How do you get around that? Juan found a genius way. He paid an FPL guy $2,000 - $1000 from him, $1000 from me – and, in return, the power guy slipped him a copy of the master key that opened *every single FPL metered box* in South Florida. That meant we could use all the electricity we wanted on the plants at whatever house we rented. All we had to do was, the night before the FPL came for their monthly meter reading, open up that box and roll back the meter so it looked like we were just using the average amount of power.

Now, this only buys you six months to a year. All the houses in a block are on a grid and FPL can tell *somebody's* milking the electric - they just can't figure out which house it is right away. It takes them a while to narrow it down. So the rule was, you did two crops and you changed houses. A complete grow took about three months, so that meant you switched every six months. It was a real pain in the butt – but if you wanted the money, you had to do what you had to do.

Later, we heard of a second way the cops could nail you. They would use heat sensors at night, which would pick up the output of the heavy-duty lights you needed to shine on the marijuana plants. We heard of a lot of people who were getting caught this way – so we just switched it up – we grew during the day. We put the house on timers, so the lights would go on the plants for the 12 hours of daylight (or mostly daylight, depending on what season it was) and shut off during the overnight hours.

At first, I would live in whatever house we were growing in. I'd wake up a couple hours before I needed to go to my job so I could feed the plants, and then I'd go to work. But it was weird living in a pot house, and sometimes I'd get paranoid about it.

So I would go stay at a girl's house or my mom's or even my grandmother's house.

As I said, it took about three months to grow the weed, about 90 days. After 90 days, we'd spend a week or two trimming the plants and hanging them to dry. Then we'd bag it up and it would be ready to go. Typically, we'd end up with anywhere from 12 to 20 pounds and they'd sell for around $4000 a pound. That meant every three months, we'd clear around 50k and split the profits.

Then we'd party. Big time.

Maybe we'd blow close to a thousand on a big night. We'd buy bottles at the club, feed the strippers and then go into the back room for lap dances and more. We also accessorized. We'd buy jewelry - huge chains, bracelets. I got more and more tattoos. And along the way, I got the diamond grill to go over my bottom teeth. Actually, I ended up getting more than one.

That was because when we were out partying, I would still occasionally end up acting like an idiot. One night, I went out with a friend I hadn't seen in a couple of years and I ended up getting so blasted, I blacked out again, just like the night with the Xanax – and I woke up all bloody. Everybody told me I got belligerent and started shit with all types of people. I didn't remember and I didn't know why. Deep down, maybe I hated my life and hated how I was living.

The upshot? In the middle of all my out-of-control behavior that night, I tripped and fell and smashed the grill on a curb on the street. So hard that I had to end up dropping $3500 to get some sparkly replacements.

But it didn't really matter with the money we were making. After one grow, we'd immediately start another one. And, in between, we'd still make coin. Juan had cousins who were also growing in a couple of other houses – I didn't have any actual involvement with them, but they would give me their product cheap because I was the guy everybody ran to when they wanted to get their shit sold. That's because I had built my own distribution network - I had a whole crew working underneath me moving product all over town.

That's how I ended up getting the nickname of Nino Breezy. There was this movie, *New Jack City,* where Wesley Snipes played a character named Nino Brown who ran this huge drug cartel. Somehow, the black guys I hung out with turned that around into Nino Breezy and tagged me with that name, because they knew how much shit I sold and how many people I had working for me.

So Nino Breezy kept on keeping on, breezing through a lot of weed and money. But I was always aware it all could come crashing down at any second.

And one time, it almost did - thanks to the Florida power company that we thought we had outwitted. But that scam only worked if nobody did anything stupid.

We're moving into a new rental house for our next grow. Now, as I mentioned, the electrical necessities at a grow house are huge. The lights use 1000 watt bulbs – and you just can't plug those things into a regular electrical outlet. No, you have to run special heavy-duty cables from the growing room all the way down to wherever the electrical junction box is. You may have to run those cables through the walls, down through the ceiling, depends on the house. The thing was, it was a big freakin' deal and the connection to the main electric box had to be solid.

My partner Juan paid an electrician to teach him how to do it. I didn't get involved, so I can't even tell you exactly how he did these hook-ups. I didn't care, it wasn't my responsibility. The important thing is that he would normally hook it all up *after* the FPL came out to check shit out and set us up as new customers.

But this time around, Juan gets a little impatient - he wants to get started ASAP. I'm moving stuff in and I see him making the connections. I'm like, "Dude, let's wait until they come and do their stuff to the box. Then we'll do our thing." He doesn't listen. He wants to get growing.

Sure enough, the fucking next day, an FPL woman shows up.

She's at the door. I'm talking to her, but I know there's no way to really talk her out of checking the box. What's the excuse? There's rats in there or something? Juan knows we're fucked and he's shitting his pants, trying to unhook all these ridiculous wires he's spent hours connecting. It can't be done in the couple of minutes it's going to take her to go and check the outside box.

So I can't put off the woman, she walks around to the side of the house where the FPL box is. I turn and look in the house. There, on the other side of the box, I see that Juan literally has his foot on the wall for leverage while he pulls on the cables with all his might, trying to yank them out of the wall. It would be a great scene in a movie – except this is all for real and we might end up going to jail.

I turn back to where the lady is, opening the box – and then I turn back to see Juan inside, still pulling with all his might. As you might guess, this isn't the way to unhook electrical cables. Which is why I'm yelling "Holy shit!" in my head, because I don't think this is going to end well.

It doesn't.

There's a giant BOOM!

I see a giant spark shoot out of the box. It doesn't fry the FPL lady, thank God, but it definitely takes a couple of years off her life as she freaks and jumps back in horror.

I look back inside. As I guess, the spark came from Juan finally succeeding. The ripped wires are on the ground. So now, we have to explain this. Because the FPL lady is shook up and wants answers. She marches inside to see what happened – and she sees the smoking, mangled mess of cables on the floor, cables that lead to god knows where else in the house.

She gives us a look. We give her one back. The first rule in these situations is keep your cool, like nothing happened.

Our cover story is the obvious choice - blame somebody else. "Hey, we just moved in here," we say. "Literally just today. We were just bringing our stuff in here. It must have been whoever was in here before us."

She sees our moving boxes. She knows that part isn't a lie. And she buys it.

"Wow," she says, relaxing around us. "You've got to be careful with this stuff." She finishes up and leaves. We don't get caught.

But it takes a couple minutes for my heartbeat to get back to normal.

This was exactly the kind of disaster I had always feared. It was why I knew I couldn't do this kind of thing forever. I wanted a legit career so I didn't have to worry about this kind of shit anymore.

And that was exactly the impulse that led me to create a criminal conspiracy on a much more massive scale.

That's America.

Chapter 4: Gabriel and Peter

A fucking $30,000 dog collar.

Two guys had just walked into the Puppy Boutique where I worked – and they were about to change my life forever. And they had just bought a fucking $30,000 dog collar.

Let's back up so you know what was going on with me at this point.

I was 24 and had been doing the vet tech thing for a few years, in addition to my main source of income, which was still growing and selling pot. But, like I said, I always liked to have a legit job going. At this point, though, I was older and I was getting tired of dogs biting and scratching me. I was ready to rejoin the human race, at least as far as my day job went – I wanted to be around people more and do something else instead of being regarded as one of the animals.

Unfortunately, for the time being, I was still stuck with the pups. The only job I found was at a Puppy Boutique store near Fort Lauderdale. They specialized in teacup puppies – little Yorkies and other small dog breeds that, when young, could literally fit into teacups – as well as lot of expensive accessories for the pooches.

So I was still mainly with the animals. I came in at 6 and treated puppies that might be sick and did maintenance on the rest. The sales girls came in between 9 and 10 – and one of them, who I'll call the Redhead, was really hot, hot as can be. She ran the floor at the Puppy Boutique. Me and the Redhead, we had a thing going at that time. A lot of the time, she'd come in early when I did – and we'd fuck in the bathroom in back of the store. And, since it seemed appropriate, we'd do it doggy-style.

At the same time, I also had a thing going with another woman who I'll call Laura, who I met around the same time; she worked in the vet's office that the Puppy Boutique used to treat their dogs. Since I took care of the Redhead at the store, I would crash with Laura at night, either at my place or hers.

For the next 8 years, I kind of bounced back and forth between the two of them. I would be with one for a couple months, and then the other one for a couple of months. They knew about it, but they knew it was the lifestyle I lived. I was selling drugs, I was clear that I wasn't gonna change, that I do what I do. If you don't like it, get the fuck out of here. That's the kind of attitude I had at that time.

Anyway, I had been at the Puppy Boutique for a year and a half or so. And, like I said, they don't just sell these purse dogs, they also sell all the products people buy to pamper the pooches with. Dog beds, dog clothes, diamond dog chains…

…and yeah, the $30,000 collar that the two rich fucks bought. They were very slick – and they were obviously gay. I don't have any problem with gay people, but you could tell these two were a couple just by looking at them.

The main one, the "husband" in the relationship, was somebody I'll call Gabriel Warhol. He seemed like any ordinary guy who had too much money on his hands. He dressed in the best - Louis Vuitton suit, head to toe, Gucci glasses, and so on. Top dollar designer stuff. His partner, who I'll call Peter Wilcox, was more the "wife." He was much more effeminate, down to the way he talked, and he wore tight little jeans and his blonde hair down over the one side of his face, kind of like Andy Warhol used to wear it. They were in their fifties and, like I said, threw money around like water when they came into the store.

As a matter of fact, they threw so much money around that some kind of *Lifestyles of the Rich and Famous* camera crew came in and followed them around buying shit. They had to shut down the store for a few hours for this production. Me, I didn't know anything about it – especially since the owner had me go run and hide in the back while this was going on. Yeah, I was still only good enough for the animals. As a matter of fact, the boss made me wear long sleeves to work so my tats weren't so obvious, and tried to keep me away from the customers. So the job switch really wasn't making a difference for me.

Anyway, Gabriel and Peter bought dogs from us and I was taking care of them for a couple of weeks. They were coming into the store almost every other day to check on them and also to buy more puppy products, because the Redhead worked them every time they showed up – she would show them something else she was pretty sure they'd buy. She was awesome at sales.

And these two didn't mind her constantly trying to sell them shit. If anything, they took a real shine to her. They were in love with her, as much as two gay guys could be in love with a woman.

As a matter of fact, they were so smitten by her that they offered her a job. What kind of job? Who knows? They didn't give her a whole lot of details, they just asked her, "Do you want to make more money? Give us a call whenever you're ready. We don't want to pull you away from this job." Yeah, that last part cracked me up. "I don't want to pull you away from your job." But you're still offering the fucking job, c'mon! Anyway, they gave her their card and told her to call whenever.

Me, however? They could give a crap.

I was low level, the guy with the tattoos who took care of the dogs. To them, I'm not worth the time of the day. It wasn't that they were nasty to me or anything. They always seemed nice. But they never really tried to have a real conversation with me.

That was how it was going at the store in general. I was still the outcast, still the guy nobody wanted to put out front, still stuck back with the animals. It was pretty obvious that Puppy Boutique wasn't going to be my long-range career plan (if it's anybody's). Besides how I was treated, I also was only working a few hours a day. My day started in the early morning, when I took care of all the dogs. A little after the store opened, the owner would send me home, and I'd go back to wherever I was growing and hang out. I'd smoke, trim the plants, or some other bullshit. Then I'd go back at 2 or 3 in the afternoon to do more doggy daycare – I'd feed the pups, bathe them if they needed it, clean up their cages, whatever had to be done.

It was easy, but it was fucking boring and tiring after a while. Plus I was making so much more money growing, it was insane and that got to me. I needed something that would pay me a real salary, real benefits and enable me to have a real life. Despite my wild lifestyle, I still wanted to have a family someday.

I turned to my younger step-brother, one of the kids from my dad's marriage after he split up with my mom. He worked for the city, he was in the union and everything. He knew the kind of thing I was after, so he got me in for a job. Benefits and everything, just like what I wanted. So I quit the puppy business and showed up for work. Turned out I was working with sheet metal at the Miami International Airport.

Sheet metal. I lasted one whole day.

I had never done construction. As a matter of fact, I never really did that level of intense physical work before. My body was hurting, because I wasn't used to this kind of shit AT ALL. So I was already not planning to go back for day two before day one was over.

That night, my muscles aching from head to toe, I went to see the Redhead. I started bitching about the job and told her that I was quitting, because I just couldn't deal with that crap.

She had an idea. Turned out she still had Gabriel and Peter's card.

She never called about the job they were offering, because she wasn't so sure about what the set-up was. So she said to me, "Why don't you call these guys and see if you can get a job with them? I don't know what the hell they do, but they have a shitload of money."

Nobody else was beating down my door. It was worth a shot.

PART 2

MR. CHRISTIAN

Chapter 5: My Life in Tattoos

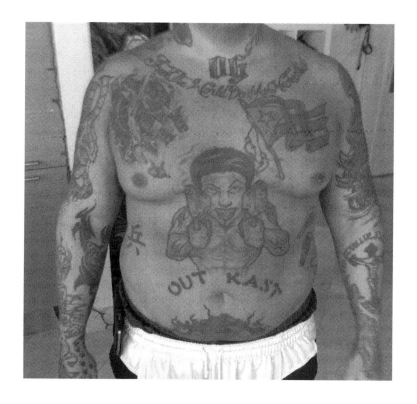

I think it's important at this stage of the story that you know more about who I am and where my head was at that time. The best way to do that? By taking a look at my tattoos.

Let me run them down for you.

On the fingers of one hand, you'll find letters that spell "Nano." That's my childhood nickname. My grandparents, my father, they all call me that. In Spanish, "Nano" is a short person – my folks thought I was going to be height-challenged as an adult, which is why they stuck that on me.

On the fingers of the other hand? Letters that spell "Nino," as in Nino Breezy, which I already explained was the nickname I got from my drug-dealing ways.

On my right arm, you'll find a big tattoo, one of the first ones I ever got. It's a big Jesus crucifixion scene with the inscription, "Forgive me, Father, for I have sinned." It's from when I was doing all the dumb stuff that got me in trouble and my mom fired. Maybe I thought it was going to stop at that point, but what it really should have said is, "Father, Forgive me for all the stupid shit that I'm going to keep doing."

On my arms, you'll also see some huge cover-up tattoos, which I got to hide some other dumb tattoos I got when I was younger. Like, I used to have Dalmatians and spots all over the place. It was idiotic, which is why I started to cover them up with big pieces. There are also some other abstract things where it looks like my skin is tearing and I'm a robot underneath. A lot of bio-mechanical stuff. But I kept some of the older tats I liked, like one that says, "One Love Going Down for Smoking, Drinking, Women."

On my neck? In one place, you'll see the word "Hustler," next to a large money bag on fire, because I was burning money like crazy back then. In another place, you'll see two large letters - "OG." Most of you know what that's about.

Around the top of my chest, ringing it like a necklace, is the inscription, "Fuck the world. Don't ask me for shit." That's the attitude I have. I go my way, everybody else can go theirs. Moving down further, you'll see the Cuban flag and a gangster holding two smoking guns. Below the gangster and down on my belly is "Out Kast." Because I felt like an outcast from society when I was growing up.

Now, at the bottom of my chest, is an Asian whore with her tongue going down to…well, you can guess where it ends up. But she didn't used to be there. What *was* there was an elephant with a crown to the side of its head, a pair of glasses with the eyes popping, and an earring. Yeah, a little elephant gangster. Above it was the inscription, "Pimping ain't easy, but it sure is fun," and the elephant's trunk led to…well, again, you can guess. But later on, I decided to switch it up.

On my back? You'll see an eye on top, watching my back. Underneath that, in big letters, is "Dirty South" from shoulder to shoulder, because, obviously, that's where I live. Then, underneath *that* is a map of Florida, huge, with a bunch of bullet holes around it and in it. I was going to do something else with that Florida image, but, after somebody close to me died, I put on an "R.I.P." inside the state with the person's name. That represents the tragedy I spoke of earlier, the tragedy that led me to finally rethink my life.

There's also some more bio-mechanical robot detail on my back. That whole concept was important to me, because I felt like I was a robot to the rest of society. No matter what I did, I always worked. I was a slave for the establishment. That's the role most of us play in our adult lives. Unless you're rich, you're a robot working for somebody else and you have to perform your duties like some kind of machine.

Or a slave.

In fact, I was about to become a slave for Gabriel and Peter - a slave who never got what he deserved and, instead, had to grab it for himself when they weren't looking. I may have thought of myself as a robot, but, when push came to shove, I really wasn't willing to assume the position.

This robot would reprogram itself.

Chapter 6: MA

I had Gabriel and Peter's card that the Redhead had given me – but I didn't call right away. I wasn't feeling good that it would actually lead anywhere.

First of all, they were after the Redhead, not me. And they had made it clear in the past that they didn't think I was worth a second look. Second of all, I most likely didn't look the part of what they were looking for, whatever that part might be. Finally, my background was pretty sketchy – I had arrests and there was that business about me getting kicked out of high school. So yeah, it seemed like my chances of getting whatever they were offering were pretty low.

But, then again, I was unemployed. I had bailed on the union gig my brother had arranged and I was done with the Puppy Boutique. So what other choices did I really have? None.

I called the number.

The voice on the other end wasn't Gabriel's or Peter's. Instead, it was some guy who said he was their office manager. He was a nice white kid around my age, I'll call him Jimmy. Jimmy obviously didn't know me from Adam, so I explained why I was calling, again feeling sure I would get shot down. But, to my surprise, Jimmy wanted me to come in - *right away* - for an interview.

Huh. Maybe this would work out.

I went to the address he gave me – it was in the Fort Lauderdale area, so the location was close, which was good. Not only that, but I was pleasantly surprised to see that the office was in a three-story professional building, the kind filled with medical and dental practices you might see in any town anywhere. Upscale. Another good sign.

The office was on the bottom floor and it was a pain management clinic. Again, I didn't know anything about this industry or what was going on with it at that time in Florida. It was October, 2004, and alarm bells were just starting to ring. The volume of prescription pills handed out by clinics like these was growing and growing, but still not completely out of control.

Anyway, I didn't know anything about it, I didn't keep track of this shit. All I knew was I had walked into what seemed to be a normal, respectable clinic. The only weird part seemed to be the patients. First of all, there were a lot more of them than you would usually see in the waiting area of a place like this – it was packed with people. Second of all, a lot of them didn't seem like the kind of people you'd ordinarily see hanging out here – too many gold chains and gold teeth.

I went to the reception desk, asked for Jimmy and a couple of minutes later, I was sitting across the desk from him. He seemed nice and professional, and my appearance didn't throw him. Another good sign.

But then, a little into our talk, he smelled the pot on me.

Back then, it was hard to miss. When you're in the growing room feeding the bushes, when you rub against the plants constantly, when you're cutting and trimming them on a daily basis, you can't help but get the oil on you and, shit, does it *smell*.

And that smell was made worse by the fact that I was also smoking it so much. Basically, you could be excused for thinking I was carrying a pound of grass under my jacket at all times. Unfortunately, there was just nothing I could do about the stink. I could put on all the cologne in the world and it wouldn't matter. I'd still smell more like dope than Aramis.

That's why Jimmy said, "Man, I smell marijuana, is that you?" What could I say? Since he was a young guy, I figured I might as well be straight with him. I told him, "Look, I have another 'job.' I sell marijuana on the side. That's how I make my real money."

End of interview? Nope. This new piece of information didn't faze him in the least. No, instead, the doors flew open. I was in. Not only was I hired – but he wanted me to start *that day*.

So, let's review. A tough guy with diamond teeth and tattoos walks into a medical clinic reeking of dope. And he immediately gets put to work. WTF. Question marks should have been swirling in my head, but I was too happy to get the job. It seemed as if finally I was getting the chance to hold down a decent full-time job at a decent business. And maybe, just maybe, it would be a career that would stick and I could build on.

So yeah, I worked that same day, was happy to do it. My actual job? Well, I was doing with people what I used to do with dogs – prepping them for their doctor visits. My experience, even though it was with of the four-legged variety of patient, had obviously weighed in my favor. It was easy work, or so I thought. I'd weigh the patients, take their temperature, check their vitals, review their paper work, give them a drug test if need be, and so forth. I was officially an MA, a Medical Assistant. And nobody was biting or scratching me.

At least not yet.

Again, it seemed like a pretty normal operation. We had anywhere from 2 to 5 doctors seeing patients on any given day and a support staff of around 15. A few girls worked the front reception desk, there were a few other MAs like me, a few managers running around, and there were people to directly assist the doctors.

And one more very important feature - our own on-site dispensary. For the convenience of the patients. Once they got their prescriptions, they could get their pills right there in our offices. Handy, right?

All in all, it seemed like a sweet deal - a real position in a real medical clinic. But as the days progressed, I started to see why I *really* got hired. First of all, the other MA in the office was a tough black ghetto chick who also had tattoos. She was a complete hard ass with a lot of the patients – and talked to them in a way you didn't hear in other doctor's offices. Usually, everyone in a medical clinic is talking in a professional way, being respectful and nice.

But this woman?

She would yell at patients, saying stuff like, "You can't fucking do that!" and throwing in all kinds of street talk you'd never normally hear from somebody working in a medical practice. But it wasn't out of nowhere – because some of the patients were actually asking for that kind of treatment. They acted like fucking *children*, always acting up and being rude and disrespectful. They lied, they seemed messed up and they went totally batshit when they didn't get the pills they thought they were due. I realized these patients were almost all fucking drug addicts and they wanted their fix. And they wanted it NOW. So they would just do whatever they could to scare us, intimidate us or just sweet talk us – whatever it took to get past us and get the pills they were after.

With that kind of situation, we *couldn't* just be MA's - we also had to be bouncers and doormen, gatekeepers who had to stand up to these idiots and throw them out if necessary. The kind of person who would normally have my kind of job just wouldn't cut it in this clinic. You couldn't put a namby-pamby college graduate in my role. You needed someone with street knowledge and a nutsack to be able to deal with these kinds of people. So, yeah, the real reason I was hired was because they saw me as the kind of thug that could handle other thugs.

In other words, I was once again hired to deal with animals.

If the patients were freaky, so was the office itself. The clinic didn't take any medical insurance – a visit was $300 cash and that was it. Also, we were told to get people in and out as quickly as possible. That didn't make sense to me. I mean, when you went to the doctor's office for an appointment, the MD would almost always have you sitting around on your ass for an hour before you even got into the examination room – and then, you would sit around on your ass for *another* hour. That was standard operating procedure, I thought.

So why did they want it to be different here?

Finally, it all started to come to me as I looked deeper and deeper into the place. Management wanted the patients moved in and out as fast as possible not out of consideration for the patients, but so the clinic *could make as much money as possible.* They began telling me over and over, "We don't want to see any of these doctors sitting here with no patient in front of them. There better be patients in their offices. If there's one already in there, line up the next few and make sure they're ready to go. Get them done."

So I got it done. I had heard that was why other MAs had gotten fired in the past – they didn't work as hard as they should have. They were hanging out, not focusing on what needed to be done, because they weren't that serious about the job. Knowing that, I put all my effort into making things run smoothly. I made sure no doctor was ever sitting by himself at a desk. He'd be seeing one patient and I'd have his next four lined up – their folders would be sitting in a wall holder right outside his door, all in order. When he got done with one, he just had to come out, pick up the next folder, and call for that patient. It was the kind of system that made the clinic look less like a doctor's office and more like the DMV or the deli counter at the grocery store. You got your number and you waited for it to be called.

But that's how they wanted it and that's what I made sure happened. I'm a strong Latin male and I step up. My attitude is, as long as you're good to me, I'm going to meet my responsibilities to you and then some. Here, I was making 10 or so bucks an hour, getting a full-time wage, which was already way better than any other work situation I ever had - that was legal, anyway. So I was ready to do whatever these guys asked me to do. As long as you took care of me, you could have said "Hey, scrub the floor with a toothbrush" and I would've probably done that shit. No problem.

As far as I was concerned, the rest of what was going on was none of my business. And that's how I acted.

But my eyes were wide open. I couldn't help but notice what this operation was all about. It was a little self-contained one-stop-shop pill store. The patients would see their doctor, get their scrips and come right over to our dispensary to get their pills, no muss, no fuss. And no outside pharmacy to get suspicious or anybody else for that matter - as I said, Florida wasn't keeping track of any of these drugs. Good thing, because if anybody on the outside had been keeping track…well, fuck.

I found out for myself how out of hand it was. Since this was my first job as an MA, I'd go through patients' folders on my own to see what I could learn. I found out all about MRIs and herniated discs. I saw how often people were coming in for trumped-up ailments. And I also saw just how high the pill volume was becoming.

For instance, there was the 180-pound guy who got prescribed 500 Roxicodone pills.

Now, Roxicodone is basically heroin in a pill. It's a narcotic pain reliever. Oxy is the same kind of thing. They both give you an instant and incredible high. They're so powerful even right-wing titan Rush Limbaugh got hooked and was arrested for his habit in 2006.

And some guy's being allowed to take home 500 of these???

And 300 Percs and 200 Oxys to boot??

In my mind, I'm like, "Dude, you could take down a fucking elephant with this medication. Or a small army. Why does one guy who weighs less than 200 pounds get so many fucking pills???"

Of course, I knew the answer to my own question. I was a drug dealer. And I knew that I was working in what was basically a drug hole. I was doing what I did on the street for somebody else – only it was different and more dangerous product. I'd say maybe 15 to 25 percent of the people coming in our doors had a legitimate reason to get treatment. The rest?

Piece of shit dealers and fucking addicts.

But I didn't want to lose the job. And I wasn't going to lose any sweat over the set-up. Maybe the doctors and the dudes running the place were breaking the law, I didn't know for sure, I just knew I wasn't doing anything illegal. I was doing my job and I intended to keep doing just that.

Somehow, however, I knew the weird I had accidentally stepped into was going to get a lot weirder.

Chapter 6: Manager

Like I said, at first, this job seemed like it was everything I wanted – a decent hourly wage, a professional office, and a chance to maybe go up the ladder in the practice. It seemed so good that the Redhead finally decided to come over and work at the clinic herself. She got put back in the dispensary, helping to hand out the pills.

The only fly in the soup – well, the *two* flies in the soup – were Gabriel and Peter. They still didn't like me.

When I came to work, I would wear a huge chain, big rings on my fingers and I would have my diamond grill in. I didn't look the part to be working in a doctor's office for sure, but this wasn't exactly your typical medical clinic. If I had been working at a dental practice or something, sure, I would have changed up my appearance. But when I figured out what was going on and saw the people I had to deal with? I knew I had to look as bad ass as possible.

Gabe and Peter didn't like that. Didn't like it at all. But, at the same time, I was doing the job right, so they didn't want to get rid of me either. I was getting the patients in and out faster than anybody else – and that included the people who worked there before me, from what I heard from Jimmy. If this was a junkie assembly line, I was gonna keep the line moving. And I did.

The other thing was that Gabriel and Peter weren't around very often. They would just stop in from time to time, walking in and leaving like they were the stars in their own lame ass movie. They didn't have an office there or anything, they'd just come in, check in, talk with the doctors and shoot the shit. There was one big upside - sometimes they'd come in with a roll of hundred dollar bills and hand each employee a Benjamin as a surprise bonus.

Yeah, it was clear they had money coming out of their ears and probably a few other orifices.

That became more obvious a couple of months after I started working for them, when they threw all their little workers a giant Christmas party. Suddenly, I was allowed entry to the gates of their kingdom – a beautiful house right off the water. They had a huge pool in the back, a Jacuzzi, Jet Skis hanging down from their dock to take out in the ocean when you wanted…the whole deal. For the party, they had tents set up, a DJ, raffles, casino games and a whole catered spread. Plus there were bartenders, waiters…and a belly dancer who breathed fire.

I was like, whoa. Yeah. These guys are really loaded. And it turned out, the money train was just gaining steam.

When people see an easy way to make money, they get crazy. And they push their luck, because they want to make the most money possible in the fastest amount of time, right?

The pain pill clinics were no different.

Like I said, we had a few doctors seeing patients at our clinic on a daily basis. But one of them was our true superstar when it came to pushing pills. At that time, we'd have about 100 to 140 patients coming through our doors on a daily basis. This doctor, who I'll call Dr. X, took care of over *half* of them all by himself.

Yeah, he knocked down around 65 to 70 of these patients every single day. I bet your friendly neighborhood family doctor doesn't see that many people in a *week*.

Each of Dr. X's patients would have literally a five minute appointment. As one entered his office and sat down, he was already writing the prescription for 'em to save time. While he wrote it out, he'd ask some standard cut-and-dry questions. You just had to land the answers somewhere in the ballpark of acceptable. Then, when the little back and forth was done, he'd hand over the scrip and say, "All right, you're good to go."

He was a freaking drug dealer, pure and simple.

Since I had just started, I saw what he was getting away with. I was new, so I was in no position to question what he was doing. Nope, I could only shake my head in awe and wonder. This guy was in his sixties and apparently wanted his retirement fund NOW. I actually didn't know what his motivation was – I just know that his insane greed would cost me a whole lot of time and trouble, cost a few people their lives, and would eventually start bringing the whole scam to a screeching halt.

But that was a few years down the road. For now, he was the engineer driving the money train I was talking about. Gabe and Pete loved this guy so much, they even put him on a late night commercial advertising our clinic. The thing was incredibly cheesy and only ran a few times – but still, they were nuts enough to make this sleazy sawbones the face of their business!

The truth was, Dr. X was indeed our main attraction, getting most of the patients and most of the money. The other doctors couldn't help but notice that patients were asking to see him, not them - because those patients knew Dr. X would give them what they wanted without a problem.

Not only that, but Dr. X would also give those patients more of what they were looking for. If a patient was okay getting 240 or 320 pills, any of the doctors would do that. But if they wanted to hit the 400 or 500 mark, and maybe even get different brands of medication, they knew to see the man with the heavy hand. That's what we called Dr. X, the man with the heavy hand.

I don't know what the other doctors called him, but they weren't too happy. They were kind of *trying* to be legit, but they found that their patient fees were shrinking, because everybody wanted what Dr. X's heavy hand would give 'em. Which meant *those* MDs had to lower their standards and up their prescriptions to keep competitive.

Ain't that America.

Again, I was just a lowly MA. I kept my nose down and did my job. That meant getting people in and ready as quickly as possible. Again, I was good at it. Nobody wanted to fuck with me. Because I kept control, because I kept things moving, the office ran smoother and it made more money. I had shown my worth.

Suddenly, Gabe and Pete were a little happier about having me around. So happy they wanted to open another clinic - with *me* running it.

Yeah, that's how things went at this operation. Me, the supposed thug with tattoos that had been thought to be unworthy to serve as an MA, was now being asked to manage a new clinic all by myself – after only working for these boys for 8 months.

I had to admit it was a compliment. I had to see this as progress. For the first time, I was given the keys to my own little kingdom – and some hope that maybe I could make a career out of this. At the very least, I could get some very valuable experience out of it that might take me to a slightly more respectable practice. At worst, I'd continue to show my value and make some serious bucks where I was. Hell, I was excited. A big promotion like that after less than a year? Me being the whole boss of a clinic?

Count me in.

The fact is that Gabe and Pete had to expand, because the whole pill mill industry was growing around us by leaps and bounds. Some of our patients had to drive a long way to see us – and clinics that were closer to them were starting to appear. Gabe and Pete couldn't take a chance on losing patients to the competition. Not only that, but the main office was now overloaded with people coming in for prescriptions – we needed more clinics to handle the growing herd. And there was always the bottom line – Gabe and Pete wanted to cash in quickly on what was going on.

So I was going to manage their second location. Shortly afterwards, there would be a third in Boca Raton, that I would also help set up. But my shop would be located in Lauderhill, a neighborhood a little northwest of Fort Lauderdale off the Florida Turnpike. And it wouldn't be in a nice professional building like the main office. No, my clinic would be in a storefront inside a strip mall. Right next to a Joe's Crab Shack and a dry cleaners.

The downward spiral was beginning.

And coincidence of coincidences, a mom-and-pop pharmacy opened soon after in the same strip mall. We talked and we agreed to work together. The whole set-up was getting a lot more low-rent and a lot more obvious. And I quickly found out that I was a part of that low-rent attitude. Yeah, they made me a manager, which was nice and everything – but with *no* bump in pay, even though I suddenly had a lot more responsibility and was working a lot more hours. A lot of nights, my clinic was open until 7 or 8 PM.

Gabe and Pete may have found the location, but I was the guy who had to set up the whole clinic. I got the computers in there, the equipment, the files, I set up the doctor's office (there would only be one in this location). Jimmy, the office manager who had hired me in the first place, gave me a company credit card to buy all this shit and get the place ready for action.

And I also got what would prove to be two very important and useful items – a company laptop and cell phone. The laptop was set up so I could download all the clinic's systems and patient info and carry it with me at all times. The cellphone? Well, the new clinic was going to have a 24 hour-a-day "hotline" number – which was the number of my new phone. Which meant, in addition to everything else, I had to answer it if it rang at 2 in the morning!

Short term, a big pain in the ass. Long term, a gold mine.

For the moment, though, it looked like I had been given ten times the work for no more money. And every time I would bring up more money, Gabe and Pete would tell me I needed to get more patients in there. Bring in more revenue. Then we'd talk.

Except the thing was, now that I was in management, I learned things. *Like just how much fucking money these monkeys were making.*

As I said, a patient would have to pay $300 cash for a visit, no insurance, no cards. At the clinic I was managing, we had only one doctor who was seeing anywhere from 25 to 30 patients a day. Well, you do the math and you see that's around 35k a week just from my little operation. You might think, well, the doctors are making most of that money, right? No way. I also found out that they only got fifty bucks of that $300 appointment fee. So maybe they're getting 7 to 8k of that 35 thousand. Maybe it takes another 1 or 2 grand to pay us our sad salaries and pay for the operation of the place. That still leaves them with at least 25k a week from my clinic.

And there's not enough to give me a raise?

And by the way, I was also doing stuff for the other two offices, the main one and the new one in Boca Raton. Somehow, I got put in charge of depositing all the money from all the offices myself. Yeah, tens of thousands of dollars they're trusting to me to get to the right place. Jimmy gave me very specific instructions – I was to put in no more than $9000 at one time –

to avoid being flagged by the IRS, which gets notified if more than 10k is deposited into an account at once.

Anyway, forget about that 35k a week they're making from my place. Now I see Gabe and Pete are raking in *40k a day* – the total cash generated by all three of their clinics – because, you had to remember, they were also making money selling the pills at the main office from the in-house dispensary. These are the guys who can't give me any more money. These are the guys that pay me so little that I have to grow and sell weed on the side to keep my income at a decent level. The guys who are making close to a mil in a month, a lot of it untaxed!

Then it turns out that 40k isn't *all* they're making. A little later on I find out that, on top of those giant piles of cash I'm putting into their bank accounts, they're also each getting a big fat weekly paycheck from *each* clinic – as much as one of the doctors is making!

Well, shit. No wonder they can buy dog collars for $30,000.

Then I look at Jimmy, the office manager. I didn't think he was making that much more than me, but the Dynamic Duo gave him a brand new Cadillac. Me, I didn't get a car. I didn't get anything extra unless Gabe and Pete stopped by to hand out hundred dollar bills for fun. But there was no point in getting pissed off at Jimmy. I could tell he was getting stressed out from doing what he had to do for these guys. He was starting to lose it.

Hell, I thought I could lose it. Now that I'm not just an MA, now that I'm a manager, I'm suddenly the ultimate gatekeeper. I decide who gets in to see the doctor for pills and who doesn't. I'm the monster known as the Thing that's In Their Way.

Despite everything I'm talking about here, there were still procedures that had to be followed so all the clinic's paperwork looked right. The Department of Health wasn't around much, but you wanted to make sure everything looked good when they did stop by.

Here's what you had to look out for.

When somebody goes from clinic to clinic, getting different prescriptions from different MDs, that's called "doctor shopping" and it's illegal. At that point in time in Florida, however, as I already talked about, the prescriptions were on paper, not electronically tracked - so doctor shopping was a breeze to get away with.

So, if you were a dealer, if you went around selling the stuff you got from prescriptions, you might have 5 or 10 different regular doctors you'd go to for pills, none of whom knew about the others. Then, to get those prescriptions filled, you'd be a little careful, because that's where you could get caught up. You had to avoid chain pharmacies, like a Walgreens or a CVS, because they might be tracking prescriptions between their different stores. The safe way to go was with privately-owned mom-and-pop pharmacies like the one that opened by my clinic in the strip mall; you just went to a different store for each prescription and, again, the one pharmacy didn't know what the other pharmacy was doing. Nobody would know, especially not anybody in Florida law enforcement. The Sunshine State kept itself in the dark as to what was going on.

A dealer would be more of a pro. A junkie would be another story entirely. If you were actually *taking* all the shit you got from different doctors, then you might not be so careful, being fucked up on pills and all. You might screw up and forget what pharmacy you went to and when. That's when I might get a call that would go like this: "Hey, this patient here saw Doctor So-and-so yesterday, and then this other doctor a week before, and now we've got duplicate medications of the same thing that *you* guys are giving them."

That's when I would have to do my job and get that patient out of the clinic. And that's when I would have trouble. That patient might scream at me, might spit at me, might curse at me and threaten me. That patient might even get violent – but not for long, because I knew how to handle them. But the confrontations were constant and it wore me down.

Now, don't get me wrong, some patients were nice and they actually needed the pain pills for an injury or whatever. But more and more, I was seeing more scammers than actual patients. People would actually cut and paste MRIs together to make it look like they had injuries they didn't have, it was that nuts.

But I was still determined, at the beginning especially, to make sure shit was done as much by the book as possible. That was my job.

For instance, we'd have to give patients drug tests, and not for the reasons you might think. It was to make sure they were actually taking their medication and not selling the shit on the street. This was something we had to do to demonstrate to the Department of Health that we were actually looking out for the patient's welfare.

And we had to watch out for patients coming back in before their prescriptions were due to be refilled. The scripts we gave out were meant to cover 30 days of pain – which meant a patient had to wait out those 30 days before they could get more. That was the fucking law. But there were always a few idiots who would come back early to try and get more pills because they either sold them all or swallowed them all. Or some combination of those.

In those cases, there were basically two different stories they would give us. Either they said they lost the pills – or that somebody stole them.

Well, if they were "stolen," we couldn't do anything unless they filed a police report that we could put in their file. And even then we couldn't *replace* those pills with the exact same medication. We had to give them something different that acted the same, maybe just a different brand, and then we could only give them enough to get them through to the end of the 30 day period.

On the other hand, if they said they "lost" the pills – well, first of all, it was bullshit. They didn't lose them. They sold them. Or they took them all. In any event, we couldn't do anything with that pathetic excuse. I'd be like, "I don't know what to tell you. You're going to have go try and find them or something, 'cause you're not getting any more medication from here."

Later on, I would be more accommodating – for a price. At that point, I still cared about running a tight ship. But damn if there wasn't always another mutiny lurking around the corner. That's why one doctor later on started calling me "Mr. Christian."

At first I didn't know what he was talking about, but then, I had never seen the movie, *Mutiny on the Bounty*. The doc gave me a DVD of it. It was about a British Royal Navy ship in the 1700's and Marlon Brando played Mr. Christian, the guy who was under the captain, but in charge of the rest of the crew. He was in the tough spot. The captain was a real asshole and he was always yelling at Mr. Christian about the crew. The crew hated the shit the captain rained down on their heads so they were always yelling at Mr. Christian about it. Mr. Christian was always in the middle – he either had to put up with the captain's stupid shit or he had to calm the crew down and get them to do what they were supposed to do.

That's exactly where I was. I had to deal with a couple of "captains" – Gabriel and Pete – who began to act weirder and weirder as time went by. At the same time I was fighting with the patients and the doctors about what was going on under me. I was the guy in the middle. I was Mr. Christian, all right. Trouble could start at the drop of a hat.

Or, to be more accurate, a drop of a prescription bottle.

One time, a patient dropped his pills and they spilled all over the floor of the waiting room. Holy Jesus, it was like somebody busted a piñata full of Oxys in a room full of addicts - in other words, it was instant fucking chaos.

All the other patients were up off their asses in a flash and on their way to grab whatever goodies were rolling around on the floor. And they quickly got in each other's ways. Pushing, fighting, kicking, even biting – doing whatever they had to do to get some of those pills.

I had to dive into the middle of it to break it up – that was my job. But for once, even I couldn't control the situation. Instead, I got punched in the face for my trouble. It was totally out of control - and I couldn't even call the cops, because Gabe and

Pete didn't want that kind of attention drawn to the place – *ever*. It was up to me to find a way to stop this thing and I did.

Did I mention I carried a gun?

I guess this is a good time to tell you that I did – and this was one time when I was glad, because I didn't see anything else that was going to shut down this pill pandemonium.   I pulled out my piece and threw my concealed weapons badge on the floor. That got everybody's attention. The riot broke up and everybody went back to their respective seats.

That was the kind of shit I had to deal with. And again, for no more money than I was making as an MA. Finally, FINALLY, they gave me a couple more bucks an hour, but that was nothing considering what my responsibilities had mushroomed into - and compared to what they were making off my work.

Thanks to me, the new clinic was a nonstop ATM for them. I was putting in a lot of hours and incurring a ton of stress - and all I was getting in return were a bunch of empty promises.

This became a pattern – because they thought I was easy to fool.

It wasn't just me. They did it with everybody. They had this attitude that they could manipulate everybody who worked for them into doing what they wanted them to do. They were the puppet masters – and they could make us dance to whatever tune they decided to play.

For example, they encouraged me to take shortcuts with patients who maybe didn't qualify to see the doctor. Maybe their injuries weren't quite as bad as they pretended, maybe their MRI didn't show enough of a physical problem. Well, Gabe and Pete wanted me to sweet talk the doctors into seeing these questionable patients, so they could make as much money as possible, whether it was ethical or not.

At the same time, they'd go to the doctors and tell them they should trust me when I told them they should see one of these questionable patients. The Dynamic Duo told the MDs that I had things under control, that I was properly screening the patients, and that if I vouched for somebody, I knew what I was talking about.

But it wasn't about helping these patients. It was about taking their money and getting them back in next month for more pills.

Gabe and Pete also always looked for a carrot on a stick to dangle in front of my face. They would tell me that they were going to give me stock options in their new company (more about that later). Or that they were going to give me a bigger promotion.

Then later on came the biggest lie of all.

I wanted to open my own clinic with my dad. I had the money to make it happen – all I needed was to get a doctor onboard. I figured Gabe and Pete could help with that part, since they seemed to have no trouble staffing their clinics with MDS. In return, I would give them a piece of the pie. Their names would be on the contract as our partners legally – and I even offered to continue to help run their clinics. Win-win, right?

They said sure, they just wanted to wait a little bit, but definitely, this was gonna happen.

This was the lie that really hooked me. My own clinic? My own surefire business with my father? C'mon, it was the dream. I got excited just thinking of earning what Gabe and Pete were taking in every week and imagining it in my bank account. No more selling weed to make ends meet – I would be set in a legal business that I knew inside and out. It was what I had wanted more than anything.

Too bad they had no intention on delivering on any of it. Gradually, I saw there was about as much chance of this happening as my tattoos vanishing from my skin overnight.

It hurt bad when I finally realized it was just more crap from the Kings of Bullshit. I did an amazing job for these creeps. I gave my all and I get 12 or 13 bucks an hour back. I saw it all clearly. Doctors, alleged medical professionals who were more like legal drug dealers, were basically trading prescriptions for money. Gabe and Pete were making dough hand over fist without having to do much of anything to make it happen. Everybody had a good thing going.

Everybody but me.

This Mr. Christian was gonna have to start his own mutiny to get what he wanted. And he was going to have to do it sooner rather than later. Because there was a storm on the horizon, a big fucking storm, and it was going to change everything.

And I mean all that literally.

Chapter 7: Wilma

I started small.

Like I said, Jimmy the office manager was starting to lose it. I liked the guy, he was always straight with me, but he was getting burnt out. And he was getting sloppy.

There was some cash he was in charge of collecting from the offices, but he began to forget about picking it up. I would remind him, but he still wouldn't do what he was supposed to. It started sitting around for weeks at a time in my office.

I decided to test the waters.

I took some of the cash and pocketed it. Just to see if anybody was paying attention.

Nobody was. Nobody said anything, nobody did anything and, as far as I could tell, nobody noticed anything. The money stayed in my pocket. Well, at least until I spent it.

That was step one. Step two was a much bigger one.

At my new clinic, the one I was now managing, we had a patient who was a bodybuilder, a super big guy. He saw me, saw my tattoos, saw the way I carried myself, and he could tell I was from the street, somebody he could relate to. So, when he'd come in, he would chat me up, talking about this and that. I later learned this was how people would circle you before they approached you about doing a deal.

A couple visits down the road, he made that approach. He became the first guy with the cojones to ask me, "Hey, why don't you sell me a prescription?"

He offered to pay me two or three hundred bucks for a blank scrip from the pad.

Now, in theory? This sounded like real easy money. Who's going to miss one piece of paper from the prescription pad? But I had to figure out how to make this work without getting caught - I didn't want to lose my job over a couple hundred bucks. So, while he was in doing his appointment with the doctor, I thought it through. If he forged a prescription, it would still have our clinic's name on it. And whatever pharmacy he took it to would call us to verify it. If I'm not the guy who gets that call, it's gonna raise a big red flag.

That's when I remembered our 24 hour hotline number. The one that went right to my new cell phone from Gabe and Pete. Nobody but me answered those calls.

Up until that second, that cell phone was just another thing that pissed me off about my job. I could be half in the bag, enjoying myself (and maybe somebody else) at a strip club at 1 in the morning, and if that phone rang, I had to answer it. Usually it was a patient or a newbie just asking a dumb question. Pain in the ass.

But now…

If the bodybuilder went to get the prescription *after* the clinic was closed, the pharmacy would call the 24 hour number instead of the office number to check on it. I would get that call on my cell, boot up my company laptop to double check on the patient, and, if everything checked out, I would tell the pharmacist, sure, that prescription's legit, go ahead and fill it.

In other words...*I had the power to verify the prescription myself.*

Game changer.

The bodybuilder came out from his doctor appointment and I pulled him aside. I said, "Look, I'm gonna sell you the blank prescription paper. When you go home, before you cash the *real* prescription you just got today, trace the doctor's signature. Get a light, a nice bright light, and trace that signature on the blank paper that I just sold you. Just put the same *everything* that the doctor wrote on your prescription on the blank, then go fill the real one from your appointment, we'll okay it as usual here in the office. The second one, though – do *that* one after clinic hours at a different pharmacy. Give me a heads-up phone call to let me know when you're going to do it. I'll be ready."

He did as he was told. He put in the real prescription from the doctor, then, later, after we were closed, he called me to tell me he was going to put in the forged one. I got set up. I turned on my laptop so that when the pharmacy called, I would have the bodybuilder's info up on the screen. I could give them his diagnosis, the doctor's recommended treatment and whatever else the pharmacy asked for. Most of the time, all that shit wasn't necessary, but I wanted to be sure that this worked.

And it did. It worked like a fucking charm.

It was a good day for me and a good day for the bodybuilder. I got some extra cash and he got twice as many pills as he would've otherwise. As it was, the real prescription was for 240 pills, which was crazy enough (that worked out to 8 pills a day). Now, thanks to me, he had 480.

It was that easy. So easy that the bodybuilder started coming back and buying more blank prescriptions that he would fill at different pharmacies to get even *more* pills. Which gave me more ideas for later on.

For now, though, I really wanted to make sure this scam worked – so I did something really hilarious and ballsy - I forged a prescription for *myself.* Then, on a Saturday when the clinic was closed, I went to a pharmacy that regularly filled our prescriptions and put in my fake one. I walked through the drugstore, a few aisles away from the pharmacy counter, and sure enough, a minute or so later, my cell phone rang. And of course, it was the pharmacist I just handed my forged script to. When I told her the prescription was good to go, she said okay.

Huh. This system was so good I could verify my own fake shit!

Not only that, but after the first time I put in a prescription, that particular pharmacy would trust me as a regular. They wouldn't call again. I could keep it going as long as I wanted to with as many pharmacies as I wanted to.

Now that I had a system, I started selling blank scripts to other people I trusted to do it right. When drugs are for sale that cheap, word gets around fast - so my side business started booming. Soon I was not only selling individual blanks from the pad – but I was also selling a whole goddam pad to hardcore drug dealers who would cough up 4k for one. Of course, that much volume meant a lot more risk, so I had to draw a line in the sand. I would warn these dopeboys that if they fucked up by taking more than one prescription to the same pharmacy - and that shit got back to the clinic?

It was on them, not me.

I told them up-front, "I'm going to report you, and you're gonna get in trouble for it. Here on out it's your problem, so be careful. I gotta protect myself like you gotta protect yourself."

Maybe I shouldn't have worried so much.

It was just like when I lifted some of the cash that was laying around and nobody said "Boo." No matter how many blanks I put out there, nothing happened. Nobody noticed. Not even a close call.

30 days after his last appointment, the bodybuilder came in to see the doctor again. We talked as usual and I asked him how he got to be so muscular. I had been working out for 6 years

and I didn't have anything close to this guy's build — he was so big, it seemed unnatural. That's because it *was* unnatural, of course - I was fishing and he told me what I wanted to hear. "I got steroids. If you ever need anything, let me know. I can get it by the tons, boxes."

The upshot was I started trading blank prescriptions for steroids with this guy. And I started bulking up like a madman. That probably helped feed the macho madness I would get into later.

So now I was hitting the gym every day and watching my own muscles balloon. I was making extra money from the fake prescriptions and from the weed I was still growing and selling. I had my own little operation and nobody was watching too close over my shoulder. I was starting to feel secure and in control for the first time in a while.

Then that fucking storm hit.

Most people remember Hurricane Katrina hitting in 2005 because of how hard it smashed into New Orleans. Hurricane

Wilma, which came just a couple months later, is pretty much forgotten now. But I'll never forget it. It was the strongest storm to hit Broward County, where I lived and worked, in a half century. 25 people were killed. 3.2 million lost power.

And one guy, namely me, had his life completely fucked up.

Everybody in the Fort Lauderdale area knew Wilma was going to be a ballbuster. There was some hope that it would run out of steam before it made it onshore, but Wilma was one bitch that wasn't gonna back down. On Monday, October 24th, just a few months after I started up the new clinic, after I had just started the prescription scam, she hit and hit *hard*.

To be safe, I got out of the grow house I was currently renting and went to stay with my mom and stepdad in the gated community I grew up in. I knew their house was built to take Wilma's abuse – it had the hurricane shutters to protect the windows and everything. I knew I'd be all right if I rode out the storm there.

Turned out that would be the *only* place in my life that ended up all right.

After the storm passed, trees and power lines that Wilma had tossed around like twigs were blocking a lot of streets. It wasn't safe to go anywhere, so I stayed put until I finally couldn't. I got a call on my cell from Jimmy – the main office, the clinic I started at in the professional building, was a disaster. Literally.

The three story structure was trashed. The clinic wouldn't be able to operate out of there anymore. The roof caved in and water came into the offices everywhere. It was flooded and thrashed - and I had to go in there to help salvage what we could. We grabbed whatever computers and hard drives were still working, whatever charts we could cram into boxes and we took it all over to my new clinic. The computer stuff was okay, but we lost a lot of important patient paperwork.

My clinic was physically okay, but there was no power and we didn't know when it was gonna come back on, because, again, a lot of lines were down. But Gabe and Pete, bless their greedy little pirate hearts, were insisting we open up anyway. I had to go get a generator at Home Depot to get the lights on and the computers back up. The next morning, we were back in business.

But suddenly, my little kingdom was overrun.

Everything from the big clinic was jammed into my little clinic – and shit was everywhere. Not only that, but all the doctors from there had to work out of my place – which meant all their patients would be coming there too. So now, in addition to our regular daily load of around 35 patients, we also had 50 to 60 more from the other clinic. There wasn't near enough room for all the personnel and the patients, but it didn't matter. Gabe and Pete had to keep the money train on track.

It was ugly. First of all, we didn't have the full records from the main office, because a bunch of them got destroyed in the flooding. We had to go by what was on the computer – the doctors would just give the patients what they had gotten last time around. Second of all, this little clinic suddenly seemed like a nightclub. At any given time we had 20 patients waiting inside and 30 more waiting outside trying to push their way in the door. When people want their pills, they want their fucking pills.

So tempers were short – especially mine.

I had already started to call the most fucked-up patients zombies, because they were so out of it, they would just sit in the waiting room hunched over with blank eyes and expressions. Well, now that we were overrun with patients, it was like Night of the Living Dead in our clinic every day. Instead of human flesh, these zombies were after their pills and would do whatever they had to in order to get them. I had to keep breaking up fights between patients jockeying for position.

Then there was the lady who got caught trying to fake a drug test. One of my employees caught her in the bathroom, trying to heat up somebody else's urine with a lighter so it would be the right temperature. I got called and went to throw her out. She started yelling and cursing at me and then topped it all off by spitting in my face.

I didn't care for that.

As a matter of fact, I freaked the fuck out, because she spit a goober right dead in my eye - and these people have all types of disease and everything, you don't know what the fuck is going on with them.

I went for her throat, but her boyfriend who was standing next to her pushed down my hands so I couldn't get to her. I didn't care for that either. I punched him in the face, dragged him out in the parking lot and beat the shit out of him with my new steroid-engorged muscles. He didn't care for that.

And if my problems were bad at the clinic...well, they were a whole fucking lot worse at the grow house.

When I finally manage to get over there to check it out, I see the hurricane had messed up the place pretty good. Then me and my weed partner Juan mess it up even more. The power's out there at the rental house too and, as I already mentioned, we needed special intense lighting to keep the pot plants healthy and growing. Otherwise, the plants die. And who wants to throw away 50k? Not us. So we bust some holes in the walls so we could run wiring to some generators.

Oops.

Meanwhile, the landlady's calling me night and day because she knows there's damage and she needs to get in to take pictures for her insurance claim. I keep putting her off and putting her off. First of all, I don't want her to see we're growing pot, second of all, I don't want her to see how we fucked up her house, and third of all, we're only about a month away from finishing the grow. If I can stall her until the plants are ready, it all works out.

Finally, about three weeks after the storm hits, she's had it. She calls me on a Sunday night, around 8 or 9 o'clock. And she says, "Listen, no matter what you say, I'm coming out there tomorrow with a police officer and a locksmith, and I'm going into *my* house to take the pictures I need." I lie and tell her I'm out of town, could she wait a little longer?

Not happening. She's coming.

By this time, I'm driving a pick-up and it's a good thing – I'm gonna need it. I get to the clinic the next morning around 7:30, extra early because I had a lot to do, and I have the office girls meet me there because I need their help. I leave one of them there to open and run the clinic for the day and I have the other one drive me over to the grow house. They already know what I do with my spare time.

She drops me off at the house and drives around the neighborhood, in case the cops show up. I don't want her involved. I go in and chop all the plants off at their roots and I ain't neat about it. I shove the plants in big garbage bags and throw the bags by the front door when they're full. I'm moving as fast as I can, because I don't know when this lady's gonna show with the cops.

When I got all the plants in the bags, I call up the girl who's driving my truck around and I tell her to come pick up me and the bags. I know if I can get the plants away from the location, the cops can't get me on anything. The shit that's left in the house is shit you can buy at the store and no matter what they suspect, I think the odds are good I'm in the clear. So, bada bing, the plants go in the truck and we go back to the clinic. I leave the bags in the truck while I start working.

Two hours later comes the phone call I was expecting but not looking forward to. It's the landlady. "We're here at the house. I went in with a police officer." I curse at her, "You bitch! Why would you do that?" She hands the phone over to the cop. Suddenly, I feel like my life is on the line. I don't want to go to jail, I like my freedom. It's fun out here, y'know?

The cop says, "Listen, do you know what you have going on in here?" I play stupid. "No, I don't know what's going on, I've been traveling a lot and I just run in and out from time to time. My cousin – he goes there a lot to take care of my dog, I don't know what he's up to." I make up a stupid story, what else am I gonna do?

"Well," he says, "You got a whole grow operation here," and he goes on about everything he sees in the house, yada yada yada. I mean, duh, it's obvious what's been going on. He finishes up his lecture with "When you get back here, you gotta turn yourself in."

Oh, fuck.

I keep blaming everything on my imaginary cousin and I tell him I'm gonna call that douchebag and try to find out what's going on. I feed the cop the best bullshit I got in me and hang up. It was time for some legal advice.

There was a lawyer that I hired a while back when I got hit from behind in a car accident. He was a criminal lawyer, a real guy not a storefront shyster, so I went back to him to see what could happen to me. I tell him everything I've been doing - growing pot and stealing electric. And I ask, what's going to happen with the cops? I'm thinking the only thing they can get me on in the house is the roots I left behind when I chopped off the plants to get them out. But I don't think they're really gonna pull the roots out to test them. You can't smoke a root.

But the lawyer says, "They could possibly arrest you. You might want to go turn yourself in and see what's going on."

Not what I wanted to hear. Now I had to go face the music. I went to the police station where the cop was that I talked to on the phone and ask for him. I say, "I'm here to turn myself in."

It's a moment that feels as long as a year.

But it turns out the cop's not there – he left a message for me with the dispatcher, who tells me, "You can leave. You're not under arrest or anything like that. You can go back to the house and pick up your stuff. It's out there in front of the house. You've been evicted." Evicted? That's it?

I look up and praise the Lord that I'm not going to jail.

Now my only problem is I got no place to stay. I know my mom's not letting me in the door with all those bags of pot plants, she's had it with my growing and my stepdad's still in law enforcement, so I go check into a hotel and sneak all the bags into the room. And I call Gabriel and tell him I have a family emergency, I need a week off. He gives it to me.

For a week, I'm in that hotel room having a whole lot of "me time." I hang all the plants up, I trim 'em and work on 'em until they're as ready as they're gonna be. And I keep the "Do Not Disturb" sign on the door, so housekeeping doesn't see what's going on. That I don't need.

Finally, I realize I have to get rid of these plants. They're a little premature, but still salvageable. I call around to see if I can get a buyer for the bulk of it and I finally connect with a guy I went to high school with. I haven't seen him in four or five years, but I thought he was cool back then. And it winds up being a good thing that I call him, because he's interested in buying not only the weed, but some pills I have from forging my own prescriptions.

We arrange to meet at a gas station, a big gas station that's got three islands of three pumps lined up in a row. I park at the middle pump in the middle island. There's a car already in front of me and a car pulls in behind me to get gas.

The guy I called drives up to the front pump in the front island. He's got a friend in the car. The guy comes over to my car and I show him the weed and the pills. He says it looks good, but he wants to show his friend. I say, sure. The guy takes the stuff over to supposedly show his friend. But he ain't showing nothing. After he gets in the passenger seat, his friend steps on the gas. They take off. I'm still stuck between the two cars and can't go after them.

They're gone with my shit and I got nothing to show for it.

Plain and simple, I got robbed. I left a message for the guy saying I was going to get my money's worth out of him one way or another. But that would take a couple more years to happen.

So there I was, homeless and out tens of thousands of dollars' worth of drugs. At least it was all over – the storm had passed. But everything had changed. I knew that would be my last grow – it was too risky and I never wanted to get that close to jail time again. The fact was, however, that I had counted on getting that weed money every six months and now that stream was dry for good.

I was pretty fucked. I needed to find a way to make more money from the clinic. A lot more.

Luckily, that wouldn't be hard.

Chapter 8: Sponsor

I had cleaned up most of the shit Wilma dumped in my lap. I was sleeping over at some of my girlfriends' places until I found another decent rental, so my living situation worked itself out. But I still had a big problem - how to make up for my lost income.

Since I wasn't going to grow pot anymore, I had to figure out a way of earning more from the clinic I managed. And I would have to wait awhile to do it, because we still had the overflow from the main office that the hurricane had destroyed.

All those doctors and support staff were still working out of my little clinic, along with 80+ pill-popping patient-zombies lurching in and out of the door on a daily basis. It was crowded, exhausting and intense and it took everything just to keep things together there. It would be too hard to get a new scam going without anybody noticing with all that going on.

Finally, the Dynamic Duo found a new location for their main clinic, on Commercial, one of the big business streets in Fort Lauderdale. This was a small, single office professional building right by the hospital, so it was still respectable-looking.

Unfortunately, finding the office was only the beginning of the process. They still had to get business licenses, pill licenses and get the facility set up and running - that took time. It actually wasn't easy getting one of these pain management places off the ground, despite how much you could get away with once you opened the doors.

So I had to keep on waiting to make my move.

In the meantime, Christmastime rolled around and, since Gabe and Pete had money coming out of their asses, they decided to spring for another big holiday party for the employees. Lucky us! This time, though, we weren't going to their house – instead, they leased a big party bus, with lots of booze on board, and drove us up to Orlando. They got us all hotel rooms at the Universal Theme Park and hit their CityWalk area, which was full of glitzy restaurants and bars. We all partied on the Dynamic duo's dime until everything closed around midnight or 1 am, then we staggered back to our rooms and slept it off. Next morning, we all hopped back on the bus and went back home. A good way to end the year.

Then, not too long after 2005 turned into 2006, it finally happened: The new main office on Commercial was finally ready to do business. The day I was waiting for was finally here – everybody from that office was out of my hair at last.

I could finally get my clinic back to normal.

Once again, it was just me in control of my little kingdom - my doctor and my two girls, taking care of business again. We were back to handling around 30 patients a day and nobody had to worry about crowd control, which was a big relief.

Everything was quiet, I was running shop. There wasn't anybody looking over my shoulder anymore.

Time to pull the trigger.

Because the practice was such a small business and I controlled everything that went on in there, I could do whatever the hell I wanted as long as I was smart about it. Again, I was the gatekeeper, the doorman, whatever you want to call it – everything had to go past me.

And that included every patient. I'd get their records together and give them to the doctor to see if he thought they were legit. If he wasn't sure, he'd ask me what the person's vibe was – did they look like an addict or a dealer? Or were they for real? I was pretty good at sizing them up at that point, so the doc learned to trust me. And all that trust I had built up was finally going to pay off big time.

In addition to selling prescriptions to the bodybuilder and some other people, I started bringing in my friends and family as patients. They were in the same boat as me, they worked a 9 to 5 job, but the money just wasn't cutting it for them. So, again like me, they wanted to do extra stuff on the side – like sell pain pills. I saw that they passed their drug tests, even if they didn't really, I made their records look legit, even if they weren't, and I coached them on what to say to the doc. And, because I knew the system inside out, it all worked. My people got their prescriptions. Or, to be more accurate, I got their prescriptions, at least a half to three-quarters of the pills they got from the pharmacy.

I had become a sponsor.

I knew about sponsors, because they had become notorious in those pain pill boom days in South Florida. At the beginning, sponsors were mostly local patients who were already faking injuries and chronic pain and wanted to get more pills than their prescriptions would allow. So they would pay for (in other words, "sponsor") their friends' appointments and any drug tests they needed at pain clinics.

As Florida's loose reputation for dishing out this shit grew and grew, more and more sponsors started to come from other nearby states like Alabama, Georgia, Tennessee, Virginia and Kentucky. This built up to a huge operation. These long-distance sponsors would fill a van with 10 people and drive them down to South Florida, where they would put them up in motels or hotels for as long as a week.

While they were down here, the dealers would cart them around from clinic to clinic, paying for everybody's appointments and getting shitloads of pills in the process. If the dealers were extra greedy, they'd actually pull some homeless people off the street, clean them up a little and send them in for appointments. Why not? It was worth the effort to wash off their stink and get even more medication.

After the sponsors made the rounds, they would drive everybody (well, everybody except the homeless people) back to their home state – where the dealers would make a vanload of cash from selling thousands of Oxys, Roxys, Xanax bars, whatever else they managed to snag.

Even though I had stopped growing, I still had access to weed and some coke that I could sell, so I did a little dealing at night. And when you're in that world, you hear about things.

Well, I had heard about sponsoring - and I quickly realized it was perfect for the set-up I had. Most sponsors were making good coin, even though they were working outside the clinic system. But me? *I was running the fucking clinic.*

The sky was the limit.

I was in THE ideal position to be a sponsor, because I could fix things the way they needed to be fixed at every step along the way. I could make patients' records look the way they needed to look so the doctor would see them, I could tell my peeps what to say to the doctor to get the prescriptions, and, of course, because I had my clinic laptop and cell phone with me at all times, I could personally verify any prescriptions that needed to be verified.

And if I ran out of prescription pads? I had the power to order as many more as I want – and nobody in this idiot operation would ever pick up on how many were going out the door.

This was the way to more than make up for the money I was missing. This was the way to start making a small fortune. This was the way to get past Gabe and Pete not giving me what I deserved.

I would just take it.

I started by sponsoring some people I knew, people who already were dealing one thing or another, people I knew were cool and wouldn't make problems for me. After making sure that worked, I built from there by working with some of the regular patients who came into the clinic. I was careful about how I did it. I never just came out and offered to sponsor them – I let them do the talking.

It was kind of like how the bodybuilder approached me and finally made the offer to me, without me having to put my neck on the chopping block. Like the bodybuilder, these people would size me up and think that I just might be the kind of guy who was agreeable to certain "arrangements." Every time they came in for an appointment, they would pull me aside and make small talk. And that small talk got bigger and bigger with each return visit.

They'd say one thing one month, another thing the next month, and finally, by maybe the fourth or fifth month, they'd get to the point. They'd say, "I have this friend, they were seeing this one doctor and getting this much medication and then they went to another doctor and got more. Even though they weren't supposed to. But they got away with it..."

They were, of course, talking about themselves to see what I'd say. I would just answer that I knew about people who did doctor shopping, I knew how it worked, but if those people came here and did this thing wrong or that thing wrong, I'd have to kick them out. But while I was telling them all this, at the same time, I would also be explaining exactly how *they* would have to handle it if they wanted to work with *me*, without directly offering to do it. And I would tell them that the bottom line was -- if somebody got caught at a pharmacy double-dipping with more than one prescription from our clinic, then I would have to turn them into the Department of Health.

Now, at this point, the person had to tell me what he or she wanted from me. I wasn't gonna say nothing, because what if this person's a cop with a wire and I'm being recorded? If they said it, perfect. If they didn't say it, I could live without their business.

I quickly had a steady stream of fake patients, getting me all the pills I could wish for. Just as quickly I'd sell them and make a small fortune.

And there were a lot of ways to score even *more* pills at the clinic, because of my position. If a patient had a bad reaction to the pills, or maybe if the medication wasn't working like it was supposed to, that patient would bring back the remaining pills so they could get a different prescription instead. As manager, it was my job to get rid of those pills – by flushing them down the toilet, usually – and then sign what was called a disposal contract that stated, for the record in case the Department of Health checked up on us, that I destroyed the rest of the returned prescription. Well, as you might have

already guessed, I would sign that form but keep the pills —
and sell 'em later.

So I was swimming in this shit. And even though I was young
and dumb, I was still smart enough to never take these pills
myself. I didn't get addicted or fucked up on them. After seeing
how the junkies who haunted our waiting room deteriorated
and lost their minds, I knew I didn't want to get taken down by
getting hooked on this crap. Instead, I kept sharp and on top
of things. There was nothing to stop me from getting more and
more pills, and making more and more money off of them.

Best of all, I hit on the best group of people to sponsor in the
world — strippers.

Chapter 9:Stripper Posse

At my peak, I was clearing close to $20,000 a week.

Sponsoring my phony patients and then selling the pills from their prescriptions meant I was making in a little over a week what it used to take me 6 *months* to make from one of my weed crops.

And, believe me, the pills were a snap to sell. I had my own network of dealers to help me unload the stuff. Not only that, but Gabe and Pete also unwittingly fed me customers - at *their* expense.

In those days, there would be pages and pages of ads for clinics like ours in the backs of those free weekly newspapers you see in dispensers on almost every street corner in any big city. When the out-of-state sponsors would come into town with their vans full of patsies, they'd grab one of these papers and start looking for clinics to hit.

Well, Gabe and Pete had to be competitive, right? So they'd take out their own giant ads promoting our 24 hour clinic hotline number. So sponsors looking for clinics to rip off would call that hotline number – which, of course, would ring directly to my cell phone. I got a lot of buyers for my pills that way – people would call and they never even had to come into the clinic. They just had to come meet me – which made me an easy one stop shop for them.

Yeah, old Wilma did me a favor. That hurricane may have temporarily knocked me on my ass, but, a few months later, I was back up on my feet and on top of the world. Looking back on it, it was too much. Way too much.

I became an animal.

First of all, as I mentioned before, I was juicing with the bodybuilder's steroids and hitting the gym regularly. I always had muscles, but now I was a monster. I peaked at 232 pounds of muscle, then I only would do the steroids every once in a while. I knew what steroids could do to a guy in the sex department – and with the opportunities I had coming my way, I wasn't gonna let anything slow down my action.

And there was a whole lot of action. Almost every night I was at one of my favorite strip clubs, dealing, drinking, smoking and screwing. I partied like a fucking rock star. I was making so much money, I didn't give a shit about putting the brakes on what I was doing after hours. Whatever was gonna go on was gonna go on. During the day, I kept my operation slick and secret and nobody caught on.

Yeah, I spent money on getting another car when I felt like it – and buying some sweet rims for those wheels. And yeah, I socked some of it away, putting 2 or 3 grand into my savings account every other day. Luckily, I learned from Gabe and Pete not to put in too much at one time or it would get flagged by the Feds.

But mostly, I blew my cash on partying my brains out. I was in my 20's, I was in Miami....I was gonna have my fun and make sure everybody around me had it too.

I was the man.

Like I said, my night life revolved around the strip clubs. I'd leave work, go home and shower, then head right to one of my regular clubs in the North Miami area. And once I got there, bottles were popping and so were girls' asses. We'd even smoke weed in there. There was so much cigarette smoke in these places that nobody noticed when we'd smoke our little joints – the tobacco smell easily overpowered our pot.

I'd offer the strippers a couple pills, maybe some cash, and one or two of them would go back into the VIP room with me after telling the bouncer we were going to be there for an extra 20 minutes or so. Once we got back there, they would kiss and fondle each other - and fondle me. Old school in-and-out sex in the club wasn't usually happening, but I'd definitely get blow jobs out of the deal.

Maybe I'd be there until the club closed, like around 4 or 5 in the morning. And even though I had to go back to work in a few hours, I didn't give a shit – if the girls wanted to go home with me after their shift was over, who was I to refuse? So I'd take 'em home where the real action could happen. That's where I could go to town on them and do whatever. I had pills and weed, they liked those and they liked me, and those early morning sessions worked for everybody concerned.

Naturally, I developed close relationships with some of these girls, which made me realize they were the perfect people to sponsor. They were the easiest, because they were hot and nobody could say no to them, at least nobody with a dick.

I wouldn't bring them to the clinic, I would just forge the prescription in their names. It would be a Saturday, and I'd get them to dress up all hot and sexy, like they were going in to work, and also put on some perfume so they'd smell real nice. I would then drive them around from pharmacy to pharmacy and send them in to get the prescriptions filled. I'd stay in the car so that, when the pharmacist called to verify the scrip, I'd be there to take the call. A lot of the time, I was parked only ten feet from the pharmacy door when I did it.

Sometimes they didn't even call to verify. Pharmacists would usually get suspicious when somebody that looked like a druggie came in to get pain pills. But these girls? They definitely looked young and healthy, so the pharmacist wouldn't even bother to call to verify. They'd just take in the perfume and give 'em their pills.

There was another big reason these girls were the best to sponsor. With others, I would only take *some* of the pills they got from their prescriptions. With the girls?

I took *all* the pills.

I took care of them in a lot of other ways, with weed to smoke and a few pills to take when they wanted, and I'd spend money on them at the club, so they were cool with doing this for me. Besides, I was the one taking all the risk. I was the one forging the prescriptions in the first place, they were just walking into the drug store and putting in the order. They didn't have to go through the whole doctor appointment dance that the other people I sponsored did.

So anyway, after making the rounds with the girls on a typical Saturday, I might end up with anywhere from a 1000 to 1500 pills by the time the sun went down. The girls would sell some of them to the bouncers and others at the club, and I would take care of the rest, either selling them myself or handing them off to my distribution network.

Things got wild. There was a girl I was seeing around this time, a girl I called Candy, because she tasted pretty sweet. I started bringing her to the strip club, because she was curious. Turned out she was bi-curious. She'd go back in the VIP room with me and watch the girls work on each other. And I could tell she was getting turned on by it.

So I talked to one of the strippers there that was a real badass and told her that Candy was into this. We were all in the back when the stripper started going to work on her. My stripper friend started little by little, teasing her and getting her excited. And I was like...wow. Am I dreaming?

Soon, they were sitting on the couch. Well, Candy was. She was sitting there with her legs spread and the stripper was on her knees going to town on her.

Then my friends came in and they saw what was going on. Their eyes went wide open and they just started dropping money all over Candy and the stripper as they continued to go at it.

This was way too much fun. And it wouldn't last. A few years later, a couple of these clubs would get busted for prostitution and get closed down for two years. They're back in operation as I write this book, but the rules are a lot stricter. No more back rooms. But back in the day, a lot of things went on in the club. A *lot* of things went on in the club.

And, to be honest, a lot of things were going on at the clinic. I had a steady stream of women coming in who wanted pills one way or another. One of those ways was by offering me sexual favors. We'd go in a bathroom, lock the door and I'd get serviced. Or I'd bend her over a counter and drive her home. I also made house calls. A female patient would call, I'd go over to her place, we'd do our business and I'd give her a forged prescription. Then, I'd go back to work.

Money and pussy, 24/7. I went through a lot of both of those items. Now I kick myself in the ass, at least about how much cash I burned through. But, whatever. What's done is done.

And I had a pretty fucking great time doing it.

Chapter 10: Enter Roberto

Author with real-life "Roberto"

Photo © Copyright 2014 Christian Valdes

Roberto was my cousin.

Not a blood-related cousin, but a cousin in the sense that we grew up together after I moved up to Broward with my Mom as a kid. He was a part of our Smoking Blunts Crew in high school, and we continued to stay real tight during my clinic days.

That's because Roberto always had my back.

Roberto was a big guy, all tattooed like me, not as muscular, but a lot huskier. He was also a lot quicker than me to throw a punch. He was my boy, because, if I was in a bad situation of any kind? Before I could even react to it, he'd already be rushing past me to clobber whoever was messing with me. I did the same for him - when he had some trouble on his hands, I would run up and beat some ass too. That's just how we rolled.

Now I wanted to get him into the pill business too. My other close friend at the time was J Nasty, from my mom's gated community where he still lived - but I didn't want to let him in. I was already worried about him taking too many drugs as it was and I was afraid if he got too close to this business, he'd get himself in serious trouble. Roberto could handle his shit, though.

Finally, I saw an opening for him.

Gabe and Pete still maybe didn't love who I was as a person so much, but they loved the results I got. I still knew how to move patients in and out, lickety-split, and that meant the money train kept on chugging along. They liked that. They wanted more of that. Which meant they needed another guy like me in there.

Because back at the main office, things weren't going so well. The girls they had managing the place didn't keep their clinic operating as slick and fast as I did mine. Of course, to them, the clinic was just a 9 to 5 job - I had a lot more motivation than they did because I was making so much more on the side with my sponsoring.

Even leaving that aside, though, Gabe and Pete would pop in and see a couple of the office staff standing around and talking instead of doing their jobs - and they would get steamed. So steamed that one day they walked in, spotted two girls hanging out doing nothing, and fired them on the spot. And it wasn't the first time they'd done something like that – let's just say their managerial style was about as brutal as Roberto's fists were in a fight.

But it wasn't just about getting rid of goof-offs. More and more, Gabe and Pete realized they needed street guys like me to run their clinics. The pain pill business was getting crazier and crazier. Because medication was so easy to get, patients were getting weirder and weirder. Like I said, I started calling them zombies, because a lot of them were so shut down, they'd just sit in the waiting room almost falling over because they were so wacky on pills. But they were quick to act up if they thought they might not get their medication – desperate drug addicts don't take that kind of news well.

And that meant they were making more and more trouble when they came in for their appointments. No big deal when the place was being run by somebody like me, somebody who couldn't be intimidated and wasn't afraid to deal with confrontation, could keep control and keep the money rolling in. But when it wasn't? That's when it all turned into Crazy Shit City.

So Gabe and Pete had to put aside their distaste for people like me. That's because they wanted and needed to make even *more* money. Even though they were making a ton more from the two new clinics, mine and the one in Boca Raton, they were also spending a lot more. So they wanted to open yet another clinic, a *fourth* office, in North Miami Beach, my stomping grounds.

Gabriel was already shitting his pants over this idea – he was convinced Miami was a lot rougher than Fort Lauderdale and would turn into a nightmare unless they set it up right. So he definitely wanted a tough guy to run the place. Me, I was already handling all I could with my clinic, as well as helping out at the other two offices. So him and Pete asked if I knew someone like myself who could run the new office.

I suggested Roberto.

Of course, since they didn't like guys like me, they weren't going to like Roberto. As a matter of fact, they were going to *hate* him – since Roberto was even rougher around the edges than I was. Yeah, they still hired him – he was going to start training as a Medical Assistant, like I had - but he rubbed them the complete wrong way.

I understood why. I knew how to be completely professional at work (well, at least *act* completely professional, since stealing pills wasn't exactly in my job description). But Roberto was more of a hard case. He couldn't help bringing a lot more street in with him.

Roberto didn't give a shit and he didn't care if they threw some attitude at him. He just wanted *in.* He saw the kind of coin I was making doing my own thing and he wanted to start something like that for himself. Of course, that wouldn't happen until he got the keys to his own kingdom as I had, but, for now, he was happy just to get in the door.

But it didn't take long for him to almost get thrown back out it.

I was training him as a Medical Assistant and he caught on fast. He was like me, somebody who learned things quickly and took charge of whatever job that had to be done. He was moving the patients in and out just like I would've. While the Dynamic Duo prepped the Miami clinic, he learned the ropes. What he *hadn't* learned was just how screwy patients could get.

One day, this weird guy came in the clinic. He looked like one of those trench coat mafia school shooters who would come into class one day and, out of the blue, just start blasting everybody. So that already set off some alarm bells with both me and Roberto.

This dude was a white kid, really pale, in his early 20's, and he didn't really talk even though we were asking him questions. He just filled out the forms we gave him. We had to read what he wrote to find out anything about him. Weird, but whatever.

But then, because he was new, we had to get a urine test from him. Roberto took him to the bathroom and waited outside until he was done, which was standard procedure (as a matter of fact, with some patients, we had to take the extra precaution of actually going in and watching them take a piss. Loads of fun.).

Anyway, Trench Coat came back out of the bathroom and handed Roberto the cup. Roberto looked at the cup. He saw that the liquid inside wasn't pee. Nope. It was jizz. Or ejaculate, if you want the technical term.

Yeah, Trench Coat had jerked off into the cup. WTF? Your guess is as good as mine.

Now, like I said, Roberto wasn't a stop-and-think-it-over kind of guy. Which is why his immediate reaction to the cup's contents was to grab the kid and...

WHACK-WHACK-WHACK-WHACK!

...start slapping the shit out of his face, right there in the clinic hallway. I moved fast to pull Roberto off Trench Coat, and then got the weirdo out of the clinic before Roberto decided to take another crack at him. I told the kid, "Sir, take your money, take your paperwork, this is not the office for you." He left. I didn't know where he went and I didn't want to know, because he gave me the creeps.

But somehow, Gabe and Pete heard about what slap-happy Roberto did. Gabe was already worried about moving into Miami, now he had to worry about how many patients Roberto might beat up while he was running the clinic. And even more shit went down where the new clinic was still being set up. A few days before the grand opening, somebody broke into the place and stole the computers, not to mention whatever else was laying around.

That was all Gabe needed to hear. He pulled the plug on Miami altogether. I talked them into keeping Roberto on as an MA at the main clinic for the time being. That way, they were going to keep an eye on him to see if he could behave himself.

But the Roberto incident would soon be forgotten because of a much bigger deal. Dr. X was about to threaten our entire operation.

Chapter 11: The Raid

It wasn't too long after things got back to normal at my clinic that I was able to take the trip of a lifetime. As a matter of fact, it would be the first time in my life I had ever taken a real vacation – as well as gone beyond the borders of Florida, not to mention the U.S.

And it was all due to my dad -- my real dad from Cuba.

I hadn't really had a relationship with Papi since I was a teenager – during those few months when my mom sent me to live with him, during my wild high school days. When I abruptly announced I wanted to go move back in with my mom, it didn't go over well. He didn't like what I was up to back then, and I didn't like how he judged me either.

It took time, six or seven years, for us to start talking again. He got the ball rolling by asking my brother about me and what I was doing. My brother told him I had a good job at a medical clinic and was staying out of trouble. That was what he wanted to hear.

Finally, we began communicating directly again and before long, he invited me to come along on a weeklong trip he was taking to Panama, Colombia and Costa Rica – we would spend two or three days in each place. It was just the break I needed and I was excited to go. Not only that, but this was also my chance to let Roberto prove himself. While I was gone, Gabe and Pete allowed him to help run my clinic in my place. It was a sweet deal all around.

I got my passport and we were off. It was May, 2006.

This vacation was the most time I had spent with Papi one-on-one since…well, maybe since ever, since he worked a lot when I was a kid. We visited my younger stepbrother, who was living in Panama – but most of all, we partied and, yeah, there were a few women in the mix too.

Turns out I picked a good time to be away – because, back home, Dr. X finally went down – and all our clinics almost went down with him.

A few days into my trip, I called the Redhead to check in on what was going on back at the office. That's when she told me - the DEA had hit all three clinics at once and seized all our records, including the paper files and the computers. What the hell.

"Holy shit," I said to her. "Do I even still have a job?"

Turns out I did. The Redhead had already talked to Gabe and Pete and got the scoop: the clinics were going to be open for business as usual the next day. How? Because we had an ace in the hole – our IT guy, who I'll call Phil. He and I were the only two employees that the Dynamic Duo didn't harass, because both of us were essential to their operation. Phil was a hi-tech whiz and was smart enough to keep a lot of our data backed up on CDs, which he had in his possession. Also in our favor? For one reason or another, the Feds had overlooked one of our computers – so we still had some of our office data. Between all that, Phil could stitch together enough of our systems to keep us going.

Amazing. Hurricanes, federal raids…nothing stopped our clinics from doing their dirty business. We were more reliable than the fucking post office.

I had the Redhead pick up me and my dad from the airport, because I wanted to know everything that had gone down. When she saw me, she immediately handed me the latest Fort Lauderdale newspaper, which had a huge article about Dr. X. The headline read, "Doctor Saw Nine Who Died of Overdose."

Nine people. Shit. The newspaper had all the gory details. In the past two years, nine chronic-pain sufferers had been found dead in their homes by family or friends. All nine had gotten prescriptions from Dr. X at one point or another. One of them had regularly driven 300 miles round-trip from up on the Space Coast to get pills from him. One of the victims' Moms even told her kid to stay away from Dr. X. Obviously, he didn't listen.

Gabe and Pete lucked out in one regard – Dr. X had left the main clinic about eight months earlier. Why? Well, the story was that he finally wised up about the money he could be making on his own and said to himself, "Why am I paying these fucking guys?" After all, they were keeping $250 of his $300 patient fee! So, he left us and opened his own clinic in another South Florida city.

But…he was still trying to pin everything on us.

He claimed that the patients got pills from all the other doctors that were at our clinic too and he couldn't keep track of who got what. Well, that was bullshit and we all knew it. But the DEA had to check out his story – which is why they raided us and took all our records before we knew what was happening.

But we worked hard at keeping our records clean and legal. We were careful about that shit, so they couldn't get us on anything. A couple weeks after the raid, they threw in the towel and let us know that we could come get our stuff back. I had to go down to their headquarters with one of our other managers to meet the agent in charge. It was going to be nice to get all our files and computer drives back and put Humpty Dumpty back together again.

Except we didn't get them back.

They had scanned all the paper files and recorded them on CDs. We were going to have to do this all the hard way. We had to transfer the thousands and thousands of records back into the system and print out what needed to be printed out so we could reassemble all the patients' paper folders.

Thanks, Dr. X. Rot in hell.

Except he didn't. Nobody paid a price for those nine people who were dead – nobody got arrested and no clinics got shut down. That's shocking enough – but the reason why all of us got off, *including* Dr. X, is the *real* crime in this case. Even though Dr. X had most likely prescribed most of the thousands of pills that caused those nine deaths, *he still hadn't done anything technically wrong.* At the time, there were *no* rules against a clinic or a doctor giving a patient 500 or so pain pills a month.

It took four more years until any action was taken against this clown. In 2010, the Florida Board of Medicine finally found him guilty of prescribing more than 80,000 pain medication tablets to only two patients over three-and-a-half years. Let me break down the math on that for you – that's over 950 pills per patient per *month*. Because he was on his own, he gave out more pills than ever before. This time, before the Board could take action, Dr. X gave up his license to practice medicine. At that point, what the hell what did he care? He was already over 70 by that time.

But there was no question he fucked it up for the rest of us.

The Dr. X crackdown was one of the first big signs that South Florida's giant pill party was in trouble. The newspaper article about him had a lot of nasty numbers in it, such as the fact that deaths from prescription drugs had jumped 15 percent from 2003 to 2004, killing over 7,000 people. And those were the numbers from two years before, they were the most recent ones the authorities had. It was obvious to me and anybody else in the clinic business that it had probably gotten a lot worse since then.

Still, nobody was doing anything where it counted – in the state legislature. Laws needed to change, but, for some reason, they didn't. Prescriptions were still on paper and weren't being tracked. No limits were put on the number of pills that could be prescribed.

Yeah, I was as guilty as anybody in taking advantage of this screwed-up system. I went after the money like everybody else. But when I looked above me, I saw MDs willing to sell their integrity to keep their patient counts high. I saw clinic owners hiding from the IRS most of the massive profits from their cash-only transactions so they could throw it all away on huge parties, super-expensive designer accessories and, of course, diamond-studded dog collars.

And above that whole layer were the pharmaceutical companies themselves, sending in their reps every couple of weeks to wine and dine the doctors, not to mention bankrolling their trips to medical "seminars" that just happened to be at gorgeous vacation spots. Big Pharma was just as bad as the sleaziest clinic owners – they just wanted to sell as many of their pills as they could and they didn't give a shit if they were being overprescribed. And you can also bet they were donating to political candidates' campaigns to try and keep any regulations from becoming law. Maybe that's why the state government didn't seem to give a shit about what was going on.

So yeah, between the business moguls and the politicians, the system made it so people could take pills like they were candy – as a matter of fact, they even turned their drugs *into* candy. Actiq was a raspberry-flavored lollipop that contained the drug fentanyl in a dosage that was supposedly *100 times more powerful than morphine.* The FDA only approved this thing for cancer patients with unbearable pain who didn't really have a reason to worry about long-term addiction – but guess what? Our doctors got a few of our patients hooked on that thing.

And you can bet none of them should have been prescribed the yummy numby-pop.

When everybody's making the kind of money we were coining in those days, nobody wants to upset the apple cart. But there comes a day when shit spirals so far out of control, the powers-that-be *have* to pay attention. Dr. X was the first big step towards that day.

But, for the time being, the cash was flowing nonstop and so was the medication.   More and more pills were spilling out on the streets from the growing number of clinics that were popping up in every low-rent strip mall in South Florida.

And, yeah, of course, I played my part in all this. As a matter of fact, my own personal pill operation was about to take its own giant step forward.

Because Roberto had done so well at my clinic while I was globetrotting with my dad, Gabe and Pete felt okay bumping him up to manager permanently at my clinic. Me? I also got bumped up to administrator back at their new main clinic, the one on Commercial that had more patients and more than one doctor – *and* its own dispensary. As I said, things were getting harder to control over at that place and I was known for taking charge.

I only got a very small bump in pay from the boys for this latest "promotion," but who cared? I would get a huge bump from my side activities – and so would Roberto.

At home, I let Roberto know about those activities, and I invited him to join me and do the same thing. And the thing about Roberto was that, even though he was rough around the edges, he was a talker – he could even start up a conversation with a 90-year-old lady without a problem. So I knew he'd be a natural at the whole sponsor thing. Plus he had his own dealer network in place too.

All he had to do was get the pills for them to sell.

I taught him the game – like how to make fake MRIs. All you had to do was cut and paste. You got a real MRI, maybe from an older relative that had a really bad injury, and turned it into yours or somebody else's. You just had to put in the right numbers, dates and names. Now, again, somebody like me who was managing a clinic needed to call medical practices to verify the MRIs were real. But, again…I was the one verifying, so the reality was…well, I didn't verify shit. And neither did Roberto, once he took charge of my old clinic.

With both of us managing our own clinics, it was more wide open for us to do our business than ever before.

But at the same time, we were also facing our first limitations. Because of Dr. X, we could now only prescribe a certain number of pills per month; 500 Roxys, 250 Xanax bars, 320 Percocets were all that could go to a patient at a time for their monthly dosage. It was still an insane number of pills, however, and, between my clinic and Roberto's, we could easily get our hands on what we wanted. So the new limits didn't bother us all that much.

Neither did the whispers that the state was finally going to start cracking down on South Florida's pain clinics. When a party's in full swing, you just go with it. But then the party keeps getting crazier and crazier, so crazy that you think

nothing can stop it. That's where we were.

Everything was about to get pushed a lot farther than anybody

thought it could.

Chapter 12: Patients

The South Florida pain clinics were starting to look a lot like crack houses.

Seriously.

I'd catch patients inside the clinic, in the lobby or the bathroom maybe, snorting or shooting up the shit. Outside the clinic, it would get even worse. You'd go out to grab a smoke during your break and you'd see patients in their cars, cooking and injecting their medication. And you'd see dealers and sponsors making drug deals right there in the parking lot.

That wasn't good for the unlucky businesses who happened to be located next to a pain clinic in a strip mall, usually some random dry cleaners or maybe a Subway sandwich place. The owners of these places would call the cops, claiming the lowlifes hanging out in the lot were driving away their usual customers. To fend off the complaints (and any attention from the cops), a lot of clinics started hiring security guys to patrol the mall and keep control. Our clinics didn't. Me and Roberto handled things on our own.

But it wasn't easy.

Handling patients was tricky, and it could be downright depressing. Over time, you'd see some patients fall apart in front of your very eyes. A patient would walk in looking like a normal, successful person -- very nicely dressed, well-spoken and seeming to have a good head on his shoulders. A few months down the line, the same guy would come in with holes from cigarette burns in his coffee-stained clothes. He'd smell bad and wouldn't make any sense when he talked.

These kinds of patients would turn into the zombies I talked about before – they'd be half-sitting in the waiting room chairs with drool coming out of their mouths. They might be holding a cup of java, but as they'd try to drink it, they'd spill most of it all over themselves and the floor.

The opposite of the zombies were the walkers. These patients couldn't stand still for a second. Instead, they'd pace back and forth, scratching themselves all over, jonesing like maniacs for a fix that only the doctor could give them.

Some of these patients smelled so bad that, after they signed in at the front desk, the girls who worked for me would spray Lysol all around to make sure nothing living jumped off them and infected the place. Sometimes they'd end up spraying the Lysol right on the patients. You would too, if some scrungy dude reached in to grab the clipboard from you and you saw that his hands were completely black from some unknown coating of dirt and filth.

Then there were the hardcore addicts who had maybe run out of medication a few days or even a week before. They were desperate for more – and you'd see them go through the whole range of withdrawal symptoms right in front of your eyes.

Like if somebody was taking too much Xanax. They might run out two or three days before their monthly appointment, and that would inevitably cause seizures – right there in our office. They would literally collapse, like they were a fish out of water. They might even pee their pants. I would hold them down while I shoved a magazine in their mouth so they didn't bite their tongue off – meanwhile, I'd yell for somebody to grab a doctor and somebody else to call for an ambulance. While the doctor would try to roll them over, I'd have to find creative ways of keeping them restrained. Like I'd lay my whole body over their legs and hold their hands down – because they can start flipping out and do some real damage when they're in that state. I learned I had to do this, because one of them almost knocked out one of the doctors by swinging his fists around.

The Oxy and Roxy addicts who ran out of pills early were no better – they looked like they were literally going to jump out of their skin, especially when the doctor cut them off and said they couldn't get more pills. You have to remember that with those medications, it was basically the same as taking a legal dose of heroin. And a heroin junkie is obviously going to do whatever he or she can to get more.

Patients would actually hang out in front of the pharmacy by my Lauderhill clinic and steal pills from other patients as they came out. There was this one guy I felt really bad for, he only had one leg and came out of the drugstore on crutches. A bunch of patients bum-rushed him – they tackled him, took his medication, and left him on the ground. I guess they knew there wasn't much chance of him chasing them.

So yeah, more and more, it was an explosive situation. Which was again why they needed guys like me and Roberto running these places now. It was hard to keep long-term staff people, because they didn't want to deal with the zombies. When zombies want to eat, most people don't want to be anywhere in sight of them.

How did these patients sink to this level?   Well, they got hooked – a lot of times by our own doctors who were willing to give these people prescriptions even if they didn't really need them, so they could make *their* money (and of course, with

Gabe and Pete's blessing, so they could make *their* money).

Anyway, these patients started losing their jobs and their families because they didn't care about them as much as where, when and how they were going to get more pills to pop, snort, or shoot up. When you're a hardcore addict, getting a fix trumps going to work, taking care of your kids, or practicing good (or even any) personal hygiene - everything that a normal person might think was kind of a high priority item.

You've no doubt seen commercials on TV for all kinds of prescription medication. You know that section at the end of those ads, where they go on about the side effects for what feels like ten minutes? Well, here's how that list would go for the shit our MDs were doling out:

"Possible side effects may include empty wallets, theft, lying, withdrawal symptoms, seizures, nose bleeds, unexplainable fits of rage, black pits of depression, irrational feelings of invincibility, draining of all emotion or physical energy,

uncontrollable itching and sniffing, prostitution, loss of

profession, friends and family, jail…and death."

I know I haven't painted a real pretty picture here about these patients, but the funny thing was a lot of them were genuinely nice people and they would get attached to me. As a matter of fact, when I took over the main clinic, a lot of them followed me over there from my old place, because they didn't want to deal with anybody else. I wasn't supposed to let them come over, but I did anyway. Weird bonds developed, because the drugs seemed to make some of the patients more sentimental and emotional. I used to hear all their family stories and spent a lot of time having personal talks with them.

But then there were others who were just Cuckoo for Cocoa Puffs, if you know what I mean.

There was one 50-year-old lady patient who decided to walk into a grocery store, methodically put on rubber gloves in the middle of an aisle and start opening jars and bottles of different kinds of baby food. The store surveillance system had like 15 minutes of video of her taking those jars and bottles and putting in some weird black shit that smelled like ammonia, which she was carrying in a Victoria's Secret body wash container. She'd mix the weird shit in with the baby food, then carefully put the tops on the jars and bottles, then put them back on the shelves.

And then they took her to the crazy house.

Then there was this other guy who looked like Bryan Cranston near the end of his run on *Breaking Bad,* except even creepier. In addition to his perpetual scowl, he had a shaved head, moustache and a runaway soul patch growing down under his chin. Cranston, as I'll call him, was a real dick and I already had had a couple run-ins with him. The last time, I had to kick him out of the clinic – he had gone through his monthly prescription a week or two early and was demanding more. I told him, no, that wasn't gonna happen. He didn't like that, but I told him to get out.

Now that scenario happened a lot. Patients would try to get more pills before they were supposed to and they'd try to bully you, manipulate you, whatever, but with me, it didn't work. It was against the rules and I could get in a lot of trouble for that shit if I let it go by. So that was a situation where my answer was always a "no," no matter how crazy a person looked.

And Cranston did look a little crazy. I didn't know how crazy until I was watching the news one night a couple weeks after I bounced him. The news report said that he had backed his truck over his ex-girlfriend's skull. She must have been a pretty hard head, because she was basically okay in spite of the rollover. Okay, yeah, the tire took off her ear, but she got it put back on and was out of the hospital in no time. I love a happy ending.

As I said, I couldn't get patients more pills until their month was up. However, there were other things I would do for them – for a price.

Like if they knew in advance they were going to fail the drug test – or even sometimes after they took it and failed – I would put it down as a "pass" for an extra 50 or a 100 bucks. I could make the paperwork look okay, so no big deal.

Now, a lot of clinic guys would have hit these patients up for more, a lot more, than I did - and they'd get what they asked for, because these people would pay anything to get medication. But I wasn't greedy. I didn't want to shake anybody down for serious money - especially now that I was at the main clinic. I didn't need to. I was dealing with more patients than ever before, so I had a steady stream of people willing to donate to my cause.

And for the right price, I could also fix an MRI that wasn't going to work or any other problems with their records that would set off alarm bells with the doctors. The trick was, I had to know about the problem *before* they saw the doc. Once the MD took a look at a patient's records and saw they were trying to pull something, it was all over, I had to kick their asses out the door.

Sometimes these people would be idiots, though, and they'd try to talk their way around their failed drug tests with the lamest excuses you could imagine. Like the one woman who said she tested positive for cocaine because somebody spiked her hot dog with it at a Miami Heat game.

So somebody mixed the coke in with the relish?

But that was nothing next to this other lady who also tested positive for coke. She claimed her man had a weird fetish where he liked her to drink his piss in front of him. Well, since he used coke, the coke naturally went into his pee and his pee went right into her. Simple explanation, could happen to anybody, right?

These were the kind of people I had six magic words for: "Get the fuck out of here." And I'd say them in a heartbeat.

On the other hand, if I knew ahead of time some part of a patient's paperwork was off, and the person wasn't a moron …well, I'd talk to him or her and see if it was worth the risk to make a little cash and help them out. If I thought I was taking too big a chance, I wouldn't do it. But more often than not, for the extra money, I'd make it work for 'em.

When I didn't, well…that's when the abuse would start. Or worse. One crowd came in one day and they all failed their drug tests. I didn't like them and I didn't offer to fix the situation – but they were pissed off that they still had to pay for the tests. I couldn't do anything about that, those were clinic costs and it wasn't my fault they flunked. Well, later on, they started phoning in bomb threats to the clinic to get even with me. Everybody was freaked and I had to walk the doctors out to their cars to make sure nobody did anything to them.

Even though crazy shit like that happened way too often, I usually managed to keep my cool with these maniacs. The scary part was when a *doctor* would lose his shit. It happened a few times with a few different doctors and I would never know exactly what had gone on, because whatever sparked the problem happened during the patient's private interview with the doc. For some reason, it would abruptly turn physical and the doctor and patient would come flying out into the hallway – with the doctor ready to actually kick the patient's ass. That was always interesting to see.

You just never knew how dangerous it was going to get. One time, it was my birthday. I came in dressed nicer than usual because I was planning to go out and celebrate at the clubs after work – and I knew I was going to have to stay late, till about 9 pm, because I had to count the cash for the week, both mine and the Dynamic Duo's.

So this patient came in, he was in his 20's, and he was obviously on something. He was acting obnoxious and talking shit to other patients. They started coming up to me and complaining about him. Then I caught him making deals on the phone, right there in the waiting room, so I walked over and confronted him – in a professional way.

The guy talked down to me. "You run this office?" he said to me in a not very respectful way. I answered, "Yeah, and you have to go." But he didn't. He kept insulting me, almost mocking me, so I lost it a little. I grabbed him by his shirt and threw him out. He had a couple of friends with him and I made him feel about as big as a mouse in front of them.

Whatever, it was over.

So I made it to the strip club after I finished all my work shit. Roberto and some other friends were waiting for me, we had dinner and drinks. Again, it was my birthday, so we took care of more bottles than usual. I got pretty wasted.

But I got a funny feeling as I was walking around the strip club half in the bag. I kept feeling like I was seeing that punk that hassled me at the clinic earlier that day. But that would be crazy, right? How the hell would we end up at the same place? Too much of a coincidence.

Which meant he followed me. And maybe his friends did too.

I went and got Roberto and said to him, "Dude, we gotta find somebody. Someone's in here that I had a problem with today and we gotta take care of him." Roberto thought it was the liquor talking. "You're drunk as shit," he said. I was like, "No, dude, I'm drunk, but I know this kid's face." And it was true.

When you have beef with somebody, you don't forget the face, you know what I'm saying?

I knew he had to be stalking me.

I kept trying to get a better look at him, but whenever I looked his way, he moved or turned so I couldn't. Roberto was walking around with me, but he couldn't help much - he didn't know what the guy looked like. Meanwhile I was too drunk to focus. We didn't make any progress.

I figured, maybe I was seeing things.

Finally, it was around 5 in the morning. We had a couple more drinks with our buds and then Roberto and I left. He hung by the club entrance for a minute, saying some goodbyes to people, while I stumbled around trying to get to the car. I made it there, I got in, but I couldn't quite get the door shut.

I finally saw Roberto heading my way. But he wasn't looking at me, or at where he was going. He was looking off at something else, something else he didn't like. He got close to me and said some kids were staring at him. Not in a good way.

And there were a lot of them.

And he said I should get my gun and come out.

In the condition I was in, it wasn't easy, but I got the gun. I got out and I saw the gang that was giving me the stink eye. I marched towards them, cocked the piece and shot a warning shot in the air.

That got their attention. Most of them scattered like roaches, except for three of them that didn't move.

I kept walking towards the remaining trio, with smoking gun still in hand. Then I finally ID'd the one in the middle – it was the punk from the office, the one I saw in the club, the one who hassled me at the clinic.

Really?

This fuckhead had to track me down and try to jump me with his boys just for that? I was fucking pissed.

"Don't you fucking move," I yelled.

I walked up to him and introduce him to my pistol by whacking him over the head with it. I decided they should get to know each other a little better and kept on pistol-whipping him. Roberto took on the other two and just beat the shit out of them, because he was bigger than both of them put together.

But this impromptu birthday party didn't go on for long. Behind us, we heard security coming out of the club, yelling at us to stop. We got the hell out of there.

And most of what we were feeling at that point was, thank God it's the weekend and we don't have to go to fucking work tomorrow.

Before I finish talking about all the clinic patients, there are a couple more that you should know about. They're very important to our story here. And you've already met them.

Gabe and Pete. Yeah, they were on the pills.

The Dynamic Duo would come in for doctor appointments just like everybody else and get their goods just like everybody else. And they were hooked on the shit just like everybody else. They loved to make their own "cocktails" – that was when you'd put together a Xanax, a muscle relaxer, and a Percocet or an Oxy, then wash it down with some wine or liquor. It was quite a thing back in those days.

Unfortunately, these pills had another side effect. They made a lot of users extremely paranoid. That was why Gabe and Pete would sometimes make sudden erratic decisions – or fire people without warning. They were always looking over their shoulders, because of the pills and probably because they knew their operation was on shaky ground.

That meant, ultimately, nobody was safe. Even me.

Chapter 13: Exit Roberto

I finally got a real home.

Yeah, I had stopped growing weed, but I was still living in rental places when I wasn't crashing with one of my girlfriends. But I was sick of moving around. I was getting older, and I wanted to settle down in some place that was really mine. I was starting to think about having a family and all that, and being in a real home would be the first step towards being a real adult.

I talked to Papi about it. Things had been a whole lot better between us since the vacation. He respected that I had found a career of sorts and was making it work. I even told him about how I used to grow and sell weed, but he was okay with that. He knew I was a hard guy and I was a lot like him, somebody who wanted to make his own money his own way.

And the good news was that he could set me up with a new crib.

Papi owned a couple of apartments in Sunny Isles, in the North Miami area. He had been having a lot of problems with the tenants in one of them and wanted to evict them. That meant I could live there. But it was even better than that. My dad took it a step further after he got rid of the people living there. He put the place in my brother's and my name.

I moved in. Finally, I could fix up a place the way I wanted to - and I did. I had the cash to put in stuff like a state-of-the-art TV system. And, spoiler alert, that's where I'm still living to this day.

I also kept right on earning. I was doing so well that when J Nasty, my best friend from my high school days, came to me for help, I had to listen. He had been arrested a couple times for fights and stuff, and he also had his license suspended for five years because he had a second DUI. Even though he was working steady as a welder, a lot of his pay was going to take care of the fines from those busts.

Upshot? He needed to earn more and earn it off the books. He wanted in on what Roberto and I were doing.

As I mentioned earlier, I had been reluctant to get him involved with pills because he had had some addiction problems in the past. I didn't want him to have any more. But when a friend is in need, you gotta help out. So I did.

But first I told him that if I caught him *taking* the medication instead of selling it, it was over. He'd be out and I'd be done with him. I wasn't going to see him get hurt on account of me. He said yeah, he'd be cool. I believed him. Or maybe I just wanted to believe him.

I told him to get some medical records and come in. Luckily, he had some past injuries, so his paperwork would do the trick without me having to jimmy it. He came in and got a few hundred Oxys to sell on the street to get started.

Meanwhile, Roberto was learning about life working for Gabe and Pete at my old Lauderhill clinic. It wasn't going well. They weren't warming up to him like they finally did with me. Roberto would do shit like wear baseball caps on the job and sit with his feet up on the desk. That didn't fly with them. They'd spot the way he looked and acted on the security camera video and get pissed about it. They told him they couldn't "condone" that kind of behavior.

Roberto, in turn, would bitch to me about their bitching – they were driving him nuts. I told him to keep calm and he'd keep making money. They'd get past this if he just kept doing his job and maybe quit wearing the baseball cap.

The truth was, from everything I could see, he was doing his job not much differently from how I did mine. Even though he might be a little more aggressive than me, he still was okay. As a matter of fact, unless you got on his bad side, he was pretty easy-going. Plus he was running things smoothly, no problems.

But it didn't matter. The fact was that Gabe in particular didn't like Roberto's looks. He just had it out for him and that situation wasn't improving.

However, somebody else *did* like Roberto. A patient, a well-to-do older gentleman in his 50's who I'll call Isaac, came in and started asking Roberto a bunch of questions. "Hey, are you content here? Are they paying you right? Would you be interested in another opportunity?"

Isaac wanted to give Roberto a job - he wanted to start his own clinic and put Roberto in charge of it. Like I said, street guys like us who could run these things were in demand. We could make sure the records looked nice and legal, control the crowds and keep things moving. But this was only a few months into Roberto running my old clinic - he was just starting to make the extra money from sponsoring and other stuff and didn't think he needed to make a move. So he told Isaac that, sorry, he was happy where he was.

But, as we all know, happiness is a fleeting thing.

Every once in a while you get to settle a score you think you missed your shot at. One night around this time, I settled a big one.

South Beach was setting up for the annual Food and Wine Festival, which is a big deal down here. They hold it every February. I had a friend who works setting up these events and he asked me to help him out one night. I said, sure.

There were a bunch of us, including Roberto, doing a lot of physical work, but it was fun because we got to drive little buggies on the beach to get from one place to another. But since this was the same night of a big boxing match we wanted to watch on TV, we hustled to get done – but it still took until around 11:30 at night for us to finish up.

So we headed over to the club as fast as we could to catch the rest of the fight. We were way too late – because the fight had only gone two rounds. We were like, "Oh shit." So we just hit the bar and had some drinks.

I was sitting there, enjoying whatever was in my glass, when I looked to the side. I did a double take, then a triple take. *I know that guy*, I thought. A familiar face, but I couldn't place it.

Anyway, I bought a $275 bottle of whiskey and we took it over to a table, right next to the bar where this guy I recognized was sitting, close to the door. I kept trying and trying to figure out who he was and how I knew him. And while I did that, I threw down shot after shot from the bottle of whiskey. My anger was building. I felt this guy had been bad news – and as I got closer and closer to figuring out just who he was, as I got drunker and drunker from the bottle, I got more and more pissed off.

Then it finally hit me like a ton of bricks.

I turned to Roberto and said, "Dude, that's the guy that ripped me off at the gas station. Remember after the hurricane? He stole my shit and took off without paying?" I was already getting up when Roberto answered me, "What are you going to do?"

My reply? "What do you *think* I'm gonna do?"

Then I saw he had some people with him. I told Roberto to stay out of it unless the guy's buddies decided to get in on the action. Meanwhile, I took off my chains, my rings, all my jewelry, and I gave them to Roberto's girl to hold for me. And I picked up that $275 bottle and got up to go have a talk with the dude in question.

Roberto took off all his jewelry and followed me over, just in case.

I walked up to this guy and I went, "Hey, what's up, man? Ain't you Jason?" He said, "Yeah." I said, "You remember me?" He went, "Nah." I went, "Really? You don't remember me?" We went to high school together. Of course he remembered me.

So I smashed the $275 bottle over his head and then I hit him with a left. BAM.

Now, he was a bigger guy than me, so he grabbed my shirt, pulled it over my head and got me bent over. I was looking at his feet while he kept trying to knee me – but I kept blocking him. This didn't go on long, because the club bouncer suddenly came from behind, grabbed me by the waist with one arm and around the throat with the other and picked me up.

And he carried me out of the club like I was an eight-year-old who acted up.

But the bouncer was nice about it, because me and Roberto spent a lot of money at his place. He just said, "Look, you've got to get the fuck out of here, just for the night, maybe the whole weekend. You can come back next weekend, but you started this shit. We saw you do it."

Fair enough. They got me. But I got that dickhead who ripped me off. And the night wasn't a complete loss, because we just drove down the street to the other strip club we hung out at.

Meanwhile, Gabe and Pete still wanted to get rid of Roberto. There was no real reason to, but it was going to happen.

Those two freaks did whatever they wanted to whenever they wanted to, whether it made sense or not.

We used to call Gabe "The Hurricane," because every time he came into the clinic, papers flew, ideas changed and sometimes heads would roll. This guy was nuts. One hour he wanted to do one thing and the next hour he wanted to do something else that was crazy. And neither thing would happen.

Pete usually let Gabe be the boss man in public. Pete would reveal his opinions to Gabe privately, but Gabe did most of the talking when it came to bossing us around. But if either one came in by himself when something they set in motion had gone wrong, they'd each blame the other one for the screw-up. They were the ultimate tag team, switching parts when it suited them during their pathetic good cop/bad cop act.

The bottom line was that they were both pathological liars. They both thought they were smarter than everyone around them and could manipulate them the way they wanted to -

especially people like me and Roberto, because we didn't go to college. They looked down on us and considered us stupid.

Well, if they stepped out in our world, they'd look like the stupid ones.

But they were in charge. And, like I said, the drugs made them paranoid. They kept changing CEOs to run their clinic company, why, I don't know, but they went through them like Kleenex. They treated their everyday employees like shit. Like I said, they left me and the IT guy pretty much alone, but everybody else was up for grabs.

For example, once they were watching on the security camera as a nurse put a patient in the doctor's examination room. As you've probably experienced from your own medical appointments, those rooms always have a big sheet of paper laid out over the table where the patient sits or lays down – and that paper gets changed for every patient, to keep things sanitary.

Well, this nurse ripped off the old paper and pulled on a new one. When she left the room, however, she didn't ball up the old paper to throw it away. Instead, she just dragged it behind her, down the hallway, until she got to a trash can.

Gabe and Pete freaked out. They came running out of their office, yelling about how that was unprofessional, and then they went ahead and fired this poor lady. I'm like, "Are you serious?" Yeah. These dudes were, even when they were doing the most ridiculous shit.

So I knew, deep down, that the Roberto situation just wasn't gonna get any better.

They had given me another small raise and another sort of promotion. I forget what it was all about, because I already knew at this point that they were full of shit. They just threw out titles to the point where they meant nothing and, as far as I could tell, my job was still basically the same. I just had to go help run another office.

Dr. X wasn't the only smart cookie who decided to go out on his own and make all the money himself. A few others had done the same thing after working at one of our clinics for a while. One of them who had started his own pill mill had just unexpectedly passed away. His wife called Gabe to tell him the bad news. Only to Gabe – this was very *good* news!

"Oh, well," he said, "We'll just come in and take over his practice! Can we buy out his patient folders?" Listening to this, I was disgusted, thinking to myself, "Dude, this lady's husband just died, you fucking piece of shit and you're already wondering about how to get his patients under your umbrella? What a scumbag."

Anyway, this clinic was in Delray Beach, so, like I said, they gave me a few extra dollars to go up there and manage the situation. I was working with the nurse and the doctor up there to call the dead doc's patients and let them know they still had access to an MD, without telling them their old doctor had bitten the dust.

Again, this was all about filling Gabe's pockets and using me to make it happen.

But while I was working up there, somebody back at our clinic called me to let me know the ax was finally gonna fall on Roberto - Gabe and Pete were ready to do the dirty deed. And that's when I realized that my raise was just about keeping me happy and keeping me quiet. In other words, Gabe and Pete were saying to me, "We know this is your friend. Here's some money. We're gonna give you a raise so you aren't a dick about it and so you won't say a fucking word."

Anyway, the clinic's CEO-of-the-month got assigned the job to lower the boom on Roberto. And, later, when we actually watched the firing on the security camera video…well, we got more than a few laughs out of it. We didn't have any sound, but in this case, a picture was worth a thousand words, maybe even a million of 'em.

Picture this: This professional-looking female CEO going in to fire Roberto for literally no good reason. They had nothing really to fire him for, he was doing the job. He knows this. And she knows this. So she's trying to be careful, because, well, he's a scary-looking dude and she doesn't want any trouble. You can tell she's trying to be gentle.

Now picture this: Roberto ain't interested in gentle. He starts throwing his hands around while he's talking back to her. She's backing away a little from him and, anxious to get out of there, finally asks him to give her back his company cell phone.

I'm no lip-reader, but this much I could figure out - Roberto screamed, "You want the phone, bitch?" and threw the phone at her as hard as he could. She ducked it. It wasn't gonna make *America's Funniest Home Videos*, but it was good enough to make me bust a gut.

So Roberto was out on the street. But he wasn't too worried – he still had the contact info for Isaac, the guy who wanted Roberto to run a clinic for him. Roberto called him up, let him know what was going on, and Isaac happily said, "Oh, you're available?"

They opened their own clinic PDQ. Roberto showed him the operational ropes, Isaac got the doctor to do the exams and the prescriptions. They got all the licenses they needed, then they got a location, a computer system and, voila, they were open for business.

Isaac saw the value of Roberto. Gabe and Pete, not so much. As a matter of fact, all they did by firing Roberto was make business a whole lot better for me and for him. Since our clinics weren't connected anymore, we could sponsor people not only at our own clinics, but at each other's. I would even go into Roberto's place as a patient and get a prescription for 500 pills. Their doctor was very obliging.

Not only that, but if I had to dismiss patients at my clinic for one reason or another, I'd let them know I could get them in at another clinic without a problem. They just had to give me a little extra cash and I'd send them over to Roberto's. I wouldn't put any record of the visit in our system. Roberto would do the same on his end. That's how we both picked up a lot more paying customers.

Isaac wasn't alone in wanting to start his own pain clinic. The cash was just too easy to make. At that point, we would sign our doctors to contracts so they wouldn't run out on us and start their own competing clinics. Well, the big money was too tempting for one of our physicians – he faked a heart attack and the records to go along with it. That way, he was able to legally get out of his contract with us and go open his own operation. Like Dr. X, he wanted to keep *all* the cash, not just a small percentage of his fee.

The pain clinics were now completely about fast money that was easy and quick to make. That was bound to lead to more extreme, bizarre and dangerous shit. Overreaching greedy criminals were becoming the norm in the world of pill clinics - and I was about to go into the belly of the beast.

Chapter 14: Jungle House

There were a lot of nights where I didn't get any sleep.

There were a lot of nights where I could walk into a strip club with a few bottles of pills to sell, spend all night drinking and doing whatever in the VIP room, and walk out the next morning with an easy 10k in cash in my pocket. I'd go home long enough to change and head straight to work.

Meanwhile, I was still doing steroids off and on. I was becoming a real beast. I was going to the gym four or five times a week and my arms swelled to 3 times the size of a regular dude's. My chest was rock hard and bulging. I was a muscle man with a blank prescription pad, and that made me a pretty hot commodity with the opposite sex.

Money and pussy. Most guys spend their whole lives running after one or another. Me, I had as much of both of them as I could handle.

Like I said, I wasn't greedy, so I was happy to share the wealth. I already showed Roberto and J Nasty how to profit from pills – and I even helped school two guys who would become the two most notorious figures to come out of this insane South Florida pill market.

Jeffrey and Christopher George – these ARE their real names, because they became infamous after they got busted -- were twin brothers from the tony village of Wellington in Palm Beach County, where an international cross-section of celebs and society darlings went to play. They had already had their share of legal trouble: Jeff was on probation for dealing stolen property, not to mention battery and resisting arrest with violence, while Christopher got 8 months in jail back in 2003 for possession with intent to sell prescription drugs and steroids.

But now they were in South Beach and anxious to get rich.

Well, for a while they were patients at my clinic. I can't say for sure, but I have a hunch they were trying to learn the ropes of the pill clinic business from how I did things. Back then, everyone was learning from us. People like the George boys would come in, start talking to me because they knew that I would accommodate patients I could trust, and then learn how the illegal pill business worked, by seeing how I rigged shit to get them extra prescriptions and pills. Then, they would go off and open their own pill mills.

Which is exactly what the twins did. In 2007, they opened their first clinics. Like us, they knew not to take any kind of insurance (or you get tied down by their regulations and oversight) and, like us, they only took cash.

Unlike us, though, they advertised for their doctors online through Craigslist!

And that was the problem. This new breed of pill mill hustler didn't care how anything looked. They didn't care if their clinics looked all that legit. Everything they did made it obvious to even the dumbest fuck in the world that they were all about making money any way they could.

That's how the twins came to take in $50k a day from each of their clinics. It was so crazy that employees would literally take the cash over to the bank in garbage bags! When the Feds finally cracked down on them, they found over 4 and a half million in cash in a couple of safes in their mom's house.

And the George twins didn't just have the clinics printing money. They even opened their own pharmacies to sell themselves as many pills as possible. They also took the fake MRI business to new heights – or new depths, depending on your point of view. The twins actually set up a mobile MRI center that was set up behind a strip club, so they could generate tons of fake scans for their "patients." That thing alone took in $2 million!

The fact is many places that did MRIs started taking money to rig their output too. They would start exaggerating the scans to make a patient seem like he or she really needed those pain pills. Then they really started getting sloppy. One place kept sending us the exact same MRI for different patients – same writing, identical from one to the other, just with a different name, birthdate and number on it.

One of our doctors would call and bitch about these copycat MRIs, because they made our records look suspect. But the place would say that it was no big deal, they were just using a similar "template" for all their scans. Our doctor said we couldn't take those MRIs anymore, so those patients got cut out.

But plenty of clinics would take those MRIs without a second glance, because they just didn't give a shit.

Now, I'm sure a lot of you are reading all this and wondering, where the hell was the legal system? Why wasn't anyone at least catching *some* of this shit?

Well, the fact is that the Florida Department of Health, at this time anyway, was only coming in about once a year to check up on clinics like ours. They could walk around and inspect the office, to make sure everything was up to code and clean, and then they would ask me to pull some patient charts at random.

So I would go pull those random charts…only they weren't so random.

I had a few charts that I knew were golden as far as the Department of Health was concerned – and I had them separated out all by themselves in a special section of the files. So, even though the authorities were asking to see any chart at random, they were only seeing the chart I wanted them to see. It just *looked* like I was plucking it out of all of the charts with no idea of which one it was.

That's how easy it was to scam the system then. That's why the clinic business continued to break the law in more and more outrageous and obvious ways. It was like the Wild, Wild West. Only there wasn't even a town sheriff walking the streets in these here parts.

Since there was more than enough cash to go around in this climate, I continued to help out everybody I could -- friends and family mostly -- by letting them in on the sponsor scam. That included an older female relative of mine who I'll call Aunt Tania. She was having some big money issues, so I asked her if she wanted to do the patient thing, and she agreed.

But I didn't take her into my clinic, in case anybody made the connection between us. I took her somewhere else. It was another clinic I had been wanting to check out – so it was killing two birds with one stone.

I took her to a jungle house.

A jungle house was my name for the lowest level of pain clinic around in those days. Jungle houses were places that had abandoned any attempt at trying to look respectable. Other people called these low-rent clinics DMVs, because you ended up in a mob of patients, waiting around for somebody to call your name - but to me, they were always jungle houses or mad houses. That's because the patients who went there were fucking insane, like animals or children. You had to talk to them like they were misbehaving three-year-olds, because adult conversation didn't really penetrate what was left of their brains.

At a jungle house, you'd find people immediately outside selling drugs. You'd even find people immediately *inside* selling drugs, in the waiting area, right in front of anybody. Nobody did much about it, as long as they kept their transactions to themselves and didn't hassle anybody that didn't want to be involved.

The jungle house I took Aunt Tania to was on a side street off Commercial in Fort Lauderdale. On that street, right near the I-95, there was a row of small homes that had been converted into small businesses or shops, like stores that sold upholstery or something like that. Four of these home stores were jungle houses. If you walked down the street, you'd pass one pain clinic, then about five other kinds of shops, then another pain clinic, then five or six more storefronts, and so on. They were close enough to one another so that it was convenient for dealers and junkies, who would hit one, walk down to the next block to the next, and so on until they hit all four.

Each one of these clinics had the basics, like we did – a doctor, basic equipment and a few office staff. But beyond that, these places were a lot different than my operation, because shit was a lot more out in the open. They'd ask you straight out if you wanted to pay to get a "pass" on your drug test. They also offered you the chance to pay to get your records altered so the doctor could justify giving you pain medication.

And you could pretty much get as many heavy-duty pills as you wanted. Everybody who worked at a jungle house was blunt as fuck about what they could do to get you the pills you wanted. And since these places were packed wall-to-wall with patients, they'd let you "jump" the line and see a doctor before everybody else waiting -- if you were willing to pay a few hundred dollars for the privilege, or even as much as a grand in some places.

Of course, it was worth it to a desperate junkie or an impatient dealer to do just that – so they coughed up the extra bucks.

The gimmicks designed to bring patients in were endless. One clinic paid patients $25 for bringing in a new customer. Others would offer $25 gasoline cards, two-for-one pill specials and half-price days. Basically, a jungle house would do whatever it could to make every single dollar possible from their license to pass out pills. It was a joke to even pretend any regulations existed.

The jungle house I took Aunt Tania to was infamous – or would become infamous when the crackdown finally came down. People remembered it because of the yellow awning it had out front. Also out front were patients wandering around smoking cigarettes and doing their deals – as well as a small squadron of armed security guys patrolling the place and keeping their eye on these freaks.

Again, nobody wanted any trouble that might cause the cops to get called in.

So that was weird enough, but in the back things entered a whole new level of strange. Because this jungle house had been an actual home, there was a backyard, closed in with 12 foot wooden fencing so nobody could see in (it was up against the backyard of another house where people did, in fact, live). In this yard area, the owners had a barbeque set up, along with coolers sitting around filled with drinks on ice. Patients fucked up on pills would actually hang back there and have their own little junkie picnic – I saw zombies all over the place, sitting in lawn chairs and drooling, right next to the motherfucking fence.

We're talking about the ninth circle of pill mill hell. It didn't get any more fucked up than this.

Anyway, I went in with my aunt to help her get some pills. At this time, I was feeding people in other parts of the state -- I'd drive pills up to Orlando or clear over to freakin' Ocala on the other side of Florida. The more pills I had, the more money I could make, so slipping some bucks to my friends and relatives so they could get me more was almost a favor to me.

The only problem was that Aunt Tania was embarrassed by the whole set-up – not only that, but she was also afraid she'd say the wrong thing and blow the deal. Well, there was a way around that – I just made it so that she didn't have to do any of the talking. Well, not directly anyway. She just pretended she didn't speak English. When we got into the jungle house, she would speak Spanish to me and I'd translate what she was saying to the people in the clinic. They'd talk back to me in English and I'd translate it back to Spanish for her. So she got to hear everything twice.

A guy named Vinny ran the jungle house I'm talking about -- he would later make headlines as "Pill Mill Vinny." Like the George brothers, he ran his clinics at full speed to make as much money as possible in as little time as possible. The difference between guys like Vinny and my bosses, Gabe and Pete, was that the Dynamic Duo didn't really want to deal with the fact that they were sleazeballs making money off junkies. They wanted to be seen as high society gents who, even though they were gay, mixed with the likes of President

George W. Bush at Republican dinner parties. They worried about looking bad in the eyes of their sophisticated social set.

Guys like Vinny? They knew exactly what they were up to and didn't give a shit about how it looked - which is why Vinny had absolutely no problem hosting a zombie barbecue in the back of his clinic. That kind of thing would've made Gabe and Pete shit their pants. Vinny? He embraced the darkness. And because he did, he was up to his ass in Ferraris and Porsches, not to mention luxury yachts and a beautiful big mansion.

And I was looking to get my piece of his action.

That was the reason I took my aunt to this horrible pill pit stop. I was actually thinking about trying to get a job with Vinny – because I was pretty sure my time was up with Gabe and Pete. A little while after they fired Roberto, they were having one of their usual paranoid temper tantrums and were suddenly threatening to fire everybody. Whatever. I felt safe because they never gave me any of their stupid shit – plus I had a lot of responsibility for their operation.

What I also had was a master key to their office.

I went in one day for one thing or another and I saw a whiteboard hanging on the wall. And on there, written in marker, was a list of the people who worked for them that they wanted to get rid of.

My name was on top of the list – with a question mark at the end of it.

Okay.

Whether this was a deliberate attempt to make me quit without them having to fire me, or whether they were just stupid enough to leave it out in plain sight, I don't know. I just knew I wanted to keep the money train going – and if it wouldn't be with them, it would be with somebody else.

As my aunt was getting her prescription at the jungle house, I was eyeing Vinnie's operation very closely. And I saw where my opening was. This guy needed some help straightening shit up. If the Board of Health actually did show up here, I didn't think they would even bother asking for a random chart. They just might close him down all together.

So, a couple days later after my visit, I called Vinny up and told him who I was, where I worked and how I did things. Vinny knew about me, because by then I had a reputation. So he invited me in for a meeting. I went back to the scene of the yellow awning and the zombie barbecue.

Vinny's office was right off the clinic lobby – you just had to make a left and you were there. I'm telling you this to let you know that his office wasn't hard to get to – anybody could easily walk in to see him, even one of his insane patients.

Why was that a big deal? Because when I walked in to sit down with Vinny, no fucking joke, $200,000 in cold hard cash was just sitting there on his desk as plain as day. Piled up neatly in a huge square. A little neater than Al Pacino had his cash at the end of *Scarface*, but same idea.

Was it a show for me or business as usual? I didn't know, but I knew to be cool about it and pretend it was no big deal. But the reality was that I had an overpowering urge to pull out my gun, shoot him and run off with the money. Boom. I mean, it would've been way too easy, so easy I just couldn't believe it. Dude, you let that much money just sit out there like that? And you really don't know what I'm all about?

The second thing I noticed was that he was smoking a cigarette – which also wasn't real smart to do in a supposed health clinic. But I guess if you're gonna keep 200 grand on your desk, nobody's gonna really bat an eye at the Camel hanging out of your mouth. But still – it said something.

We talked. And I worked what I thought my opening was – how I could bring some law and order to this place. But all the time we were discussing what my role might be with his clinics, an overpowering thought kept running through my mind and wouldn't let go.

"This guy is going the fuck down. He's gonna get arrested."

The money screamed it loudly, while the cigarette said it more quietly: Vinny had no self-control. He was too money-hungry, too loose, and that wasn't the way to be. It wasn't a viable long game, especially for me, because going to jail was not in my life plan. In my spot, I'm making money, but I'm also keeping order and control. Nobody's gonna get suspicious if I can help it. With Vinny, nobody's *not* gonna get suspicious.

So I didn't sign up with Pill Mill Vinny. Instead, I went back and confronted Gabe and Pete about their hit list. They got all flustered and talked around everything as usual. "I don't know what list you're talking about. Dah, dah, dah, dah, dah." They blamed it on the lady CEO, the same one that fired Roberto for them.

But they were just fucking liars.

And she would be gone soon, anyway. None of their "CEOs" lasted very long. I had outlasted them all – as a matter of fact, by this time, I was the administrator who had been with them the longest. It was still probably only a matter of time before my number came up with them, but as long as I was making my money, I was gonna stay put.

And that money was the *only* thing that was keeping me there, even though they were still promising me bullshit like stock options in their new software company (more on that later) and backing my own clinic with Papi. Bullshit that would never come true. Bullshit I had long ago stopped taking seriously.

But, what the fuck, I did make a play to become the next CEO. I said to them, "Look, I'll put on a suit and run this thing for you. I'll organize this place so you make some real fucking money. Nobody knows this place better than me and nobody knows how to make it work better than me."

But they would always hire useless suits to be my boss instead, people with MBAs that wouldn't make it to their year anniversary with the Dynamic Duo – because they had no idea how to handle what was going on in our clinics by then. For that you needed a degree in Street, not in Business. But, again, Gabe and Pete didn't want to deal with Street more than they had to – and they certainly weren't going to make it the face of their company.

Maybe it didn't matter. I was probably making more money in the role I was playing anyway. At my clinic, I had even graduated to selling my drugs right on the premises – I had my own safe in my office that nobody else could get into, where I could stash weed, steroids, coke and pills, whatever I had at the time to deal. It got to the point where even Gabe and Pete were buying weed off me. I guess it made their cocktail hour even more fun.

When I wasn't at the clinic, my car was my office on wheels. I had worked out of whatever I was driving at the time since the days I was growing weed, when I had a scale in the trunk to weigh the Mary Jane and boxes of sandwich baggies to put it in. These days, I was working pills more than weed, so my company cell and laptop were the most heavily-used tools. I would always be on the go, meeting people at all hours, and I always had something on me to sell.

So yeah, I was okay not running the company. It just would have been nice, because I knew sooner or later, the money train was going to go off the rails and, again, I still wanted to have a legitimate career as long as it paid decent money. Establishing myself as a CEO would have set me up for my post-pill career. The funny thing is that, even though I had given up on getting that kind of promotion, I actually would become the head of Gabe and Pete's enterprise a little while later. Too bad they never let me know about it.

Business was good for me at the end of 2008 – but it had just turned real bad for the rest of America, as most of you reading this already know. Real estate had crashed big-time and then Wall Street followed suit. The country was suddenly in the biggest recession of my lifetime. Me, I didn't even notice. I didn't care. My money train was still going full speed. But maybe I should've paid more attention to the national news. That way I would have learned that all bubbles burst at some point.

And mine was a lot closer to popping than I suspected.

PART 3

CHRIS

Chapter 15: Crackdown

It came down to this – too many people were dying.

According to *The Miami Herald*, in 2009, 7 people were dying every day in South Florida because of prescription drug overdoses. The year before, 221 people in Miami-Dade and Broward Counties died from an Oxy overdose, with over 900 deaths from the drug statewide.

33 of the top 50 pain pill clinics were now in Broward County, where our clinics were. 1.8 million Oxy pills were sold in Broward alone in the second half of 2008 - the numbers were fucking out of control. South Florida's pill problem was becoming a national disgrace – and all the pay-offs in the world weren't gonna stop a crackdown.

And in 2009, the hammer finally came down.

In June of that year, then-Governor Charlie Crist signed into law a bill calling for the mandatory creation of a statewide prescription database. Finally, prescriptions would be tracked electronically, so doctor shopping would be virtually eliminated. The only catch was it would take a few years to set up.

In the meantime, they found a way to pretty much shut down the party. The Department of Health made a website for doctors only. Each doctor had his or her own log-in name and password. Once an MD got access, he or she could look up every single patient and their prescriptions for the past 2 years.

Now, not only could I not forge duplicate prescriptions anymore, but I actually had to start going back through the past two years and bouncing patients who showed up as having too many prescriptions in a single month. There was no way to bypass this shit. I couldn't do my side stuff anymore. And I could only sponsor people for a single doctor at a time.

The money train came to a crashing halt.

I had to stop doing what I was doing. It wasn't because I got into any trouble or anything, it was because I didn't *want* to get in any trouble. I had my fun -- tons of fun -- but all good things come to an end, right? I was actually okay with it. At that point, I was making $60,000 a year with the company. I think I should have been making more for all the shit I dealt with, but, still, I had never had a job making that much money before. It was decent money, so it wasn't as if I was going to starve or anything. And again, maybe I was ready to settle down. I had just turned 30. Maybe the party needed to stop.

And besides, as the old saying goes, when one door closes, another opens.

Michael Flowers was around 40, heavy-set, with that New York-Italian accent you've heard in too many movies. He was a patient at our clinic – along with his brother, his mother, his father and a whole shitload of his friends and girlfriends. Obviously, he was sponsoring his own personal friends and family program at our practice and then selling the pills everybody got from their prescriptions. That was the only way you could get enough medication to sell, by bringing in your own personal army to a clinic.

I got to know Michael's group pretty well, because they had been coming in for a while and were very nice and friendly to me. They were smart and didn't give me any trouble – and they made sure their records worked. Later I found out why they went out of their way to make small talk with me – they would butter up people they wanted to do business with.

One of those people was me.

Anyway, I had just lost some major income from the pills when Michael let me know that they had a little venture going on out in California. They had a house up in the mountains – where they had 90 pot plants growing outside. Could I maybe help them move their product here in Florida?

The circle was complete. I went from weed to pills…and now I was headed back to weed again.

They set up a system to get the weed here from out west. They had the stuff overnighted and paid off an air carrier manager to let stuff slip by if anybody flagged one of the boxes. I got the weed dirt cheap from them, so suddenly, now I'm able to make hella cash off this new source. That helped take the edge off what I had suddenly lost.

Gabe and Pete? They weren't as okay with the changing times as I was.

They weren't worried about getting their clinics shut down or anything. They had State Representatives on their payroll, so they were protected. But there was no way around the new regulations – and that meant they were gonna lose money. The number of patients started to plummet. When patients couldn't hit more than one doctor in a month, they weren't showing up at clinics all over town like they used to. All of a sudden, a lot of the newbies were going out of business. And even the Dynamic Duo had to downsize.

My old clinic, the one Roberto had gotten fired from, ended up closing and so did the other satellite in Boca Raton. At the main clinic, we went from seeing 100 patients a day at our peak down to 70, 60 and, in the next couple of years, it would finally sink to 25 a day. Sometimes during the day, you could drive a truck through our waiting room and not hit anybody.

That's because more patient restrictions happened. For example, we couldn't take any who lived too far away – like the out-of-staters who came down to get pills to sell back home. At first, I would told them where the nearest DMV was and how to get a Florida ID card so I could take them on as patients, but I even quit that later on.

The pill supply also started getting restrictions put on it. The DEA starting tracking how many pills came into the state and into individual dispensaries and pharmacies. Containers of pills were marked and tracked. The manufacturers even changed the formulation of the Oxy and Roxy pills to make it harder to snort it or shoot up with it, so junkies couldn't get the intense high they were used to.

Even the Florida Board of Health woke up and smelled the coffee. They weren't just coming in once a year anymore –

now it was every few months. And they wouldn't let me pick the "random" patient charts for them to look at anymore. No, they would go through my patient sign-in sheets for the month, all 30 pages. They'd stop on a page, point at a name and ask for that patient's records. I never knew what name their finger would land on and that was the point. That was how it was *supposed* to work if you actually gave a shit about enforcing the rules. Great job, guys.

I even ended up *helping* the Feds with their crackdown.

The FBI came to me about two of our patients, a husband and wife in their 50's. Turned out they were doing doctor shopping at a crazy level, like 10 or 12 doctors a month - and then making an insane amount of money on the pills they got from all those prescriptions. I gave the agents all their patient records and they asked me to give them a heads-up next time they came in for their appointments.

That's just what I did. When the couple came in, I called the agents, who were parked just down the street from the clinic. After Mr. and Mrs. Dealer were done with their appointment, I called the agents again to let them know the couple was walking out the door. The couple got in their car and, the next thing I knew, our parking lot was surrounded by FBI agents with guns drawn, along with a few K-9 police dogs barking up a storm. The Feds ordered the couple to get out of the car with their hands up in the air. They did as they were told, the agents handcuffed 'em and took 'em off to jail.

All that for doctor shopping. All that for the shit I was pulling non-stop for the past few years. If I needed any more convincing to not even try to play that game anymore, this was all it would take.

Gabe and Pete grew more agitated about what was going on and kept looking for ways to appear as respectable as possible. If OxyContin was heroin, then Suboxone was its methadone – the drug you took to try and break the addiction to the harder stuff. Part of the way the Dynamic Duo protected their operation was to offer Suboxone treatment to patients who were obviously junkies. If we spotted one, we wouldn't let the addict see a doctor unless they agreed to the Suboxone treatment.

Gabe even agreed to it. He had wised up and decided to get clean – so he used Suboxone to cut down on his "cocktails." Pete, however, never stopped using while I was there. I was even sent out to get him more medication when he ran out, even though the stuff was getting a lot harder to put my hands on.

Ironically, the Suboxone almost got us into another whole level of shit. That's because Gabe hired a doctor who knew how to do the treatment, even though there was something creepy about him. Our patients were the ones who discovered just what this freak was up to – they happened to get a peek at what this sick puppy was looking at on his office computer monitor – Asian kiddie porn. After they complained, we checked out his computer and found out he was also visiting some really lovely bestiality sites. We kicked the animal out the door.

As the cash from the clinic continued to shrink, Gabe and Pete tried to get some other businesses going. For the past few years, they had been trying to develop a new technology – a fingerprint system to catch doctor shoppers. Yeah, they were trying to kill their own golden goose. More accurately, they knew Florida was going to eventually pass some laws regulating the pill mills and they thought this technology would be in demand. But it didn't seem to be going anywhere.

So they worked on something else. Because marijuana legalization was actually looking like it was going to happen in some states, their IT guy came to them with something that would track pot plants from seed to sale. In states where medical marijuana was legal, a lot of the stuff was disappearing from the dispensaries because, let's face it, people were probably stealing it and selling it on the street – so this kind of tracking technology would probably be in demand.

Suddenly, Gabe starting talking to me about weed. He would tell me about his trips back and forth to places like Seattle, where pot finally got legalized in 2012, to try and see if he could sell his new tracking system. And, because he knew I had sold weed, sold it to him on a few occasions as a matter of fact, he started asking me if I wanted to move out there and grow. Was that something I eventually wanted to do instead of this?

I said, maybe, because I didn't know where things were headed at the clinic. Turned out that's what he wanted me to say.

I had one more encounter with the law. But this wasn't anything like what happened with the FBI. This time, I wasn't working with the law – no, that mother was working against me. And not in an official capacity.

That led to one of the scariest nights in my life.

In the past, cops had come into my clinic wanting to be patients. We didn't want to deal with the police coming in and out of our operation, so we always put them off, never even put them in with a doctor. We would just tell them we couldn't see them.

Well, at one of our other offices, there was a situation. The doctor there called me, he knew me and trusted me to take care of shit when it got out of hand. And he said, "Look, we've got a pair of doctor shoppers. One's a deputy with the Broward Sheriff's Office and the other one's his wife. We don't want to deal with them and I need you to come over and dismiss them. He's okay, but she's a nutcase."

Gabe and Pete's latest CEO was a guy I'll call Kevin Grossman and I wanted him to come with me and be my witness to everything that went on. Since a cop was involved, I wasn't taking any chances in case they started lying about what happened in the room and try to somehow pin shit on me. I knew enough not to put myself in that situation.

Me and the CEO got over there and first, I spotted the cop, who looked like a redneck. Bald-headed white guy, kind of chubby. His wife? She looked like trailer park trash, to be honest, even somebody you might find living on the street. I would have taken her for a junkie to be sure.

And yeah, she was also a nutcase. She was trying to act like everything was fine, but she was being way too loud and way too over-friendly and fake. Just putting on an act so she could get past the shit and get her pills.

We took them into a back office at the clinic. Grossman and I sat down with them and I took the lead. I showed them the records and said I talked to the doctor and we knew what was going on, that they were doctor shopping.

The cop, he just kept his head down the whole time and didn't say anything. He knew that the clock had run out and this thing was over – and that if he pushed things, he could lose his job. But his wife didn't get the message, because she wasn't interested in messages, she was interested in Oxy. So she went berserk.

"He's BSO!" she shrieked. "How could you do this? How dare you tell me I can't have a prescription?" She was freaked, because she knew I was cutting off her pill supply. So she kept on going, spouting stupid shit that made no sense. "He has guns! You can't do this!"

He has guns?

Well, I have a gun too, bitch...

I had been thinking of cutting a deal with them, maybe not throwing them out completely but sending them over to another clinic to smooth things over. Now, I was pissed off. She wouldn't stop screaming about her husband having guns and about her hiring a lawyer to get back at us. I knew you couldn't have an adult conversation with a junkie and I was tired of her abusing me with her bullshit. So finally I told them there was nothing more I could do, this had to be reported. They finally left, him quietly, her not so quietly. To me, they had made their own trouble. I didn't care that her husband had a badge, and anyway, he had to be worried that he got caught in this situation.

My problem was that now I was caught in the situation too.

Other cops started showing up over at that clinic, asking for me, since I was the one who had bounced the cop and his junkie wife. And I had to keep going over to the other office because they just kept coming, asking for the couple's records, bringing in subpoenas and other legal shit. Since I was the point man, I'm the one who had to supply the access they were after.

Now a court case moved forward. Prosecutors sent more people over to the clinic to interview me and the doctor on the record. And the way this kind of thing worked was that they actually had to pay the doctor for his time, just to talk to him on the record. Me, I didn't get a penny of course.

So what happened to the cop? I didn't know and I didn't care, I just did what the D.A.'s office told me to do and I forgot about it. I didn't know if he got fired or busted or what. And I can't even be sure what happened a little later was actually related to this whole thing – but I have a pretty fucking good idea it was.

One night, I was driving along the I-95, going home, when I saw cop lights behind me. They wanted me to pull over, even though I didn't think I was doing anything wrong. Once we were on the shoulder, they asked me to get out of my car. I did. Then they said they had to handcuff me for my own protection.

WTF???

I was wearing my scrubs from work, and I thought to myself maybe, because of my tattoos and all, they thought I was some kind of escaped inmate or something. But they kept saying this was some kind of routine check. Nothing about it made sense.

They put me in the back of their car and searched mine. If they were looking for something, they didn't find it. They took my keys and locked up my vehicle. Why were they doing that?, I wondered. I didn't get a chance to wonder long, because, the next thing I knew, they put a bag over my head, a pillowcase or something.

Now I was really in some shit. These were dirty cops.

They drove me somewhere, it took maybe five or ten minutes. I had no idea where we stopped because, like I said, I had a fucking bag over my head. They yanked me out of the car. I think it was still just the two guys that originally pulled me over.

Anyway, they started saying all this goofy nonsense about losing some of their brothers on the force and that I caused major damage to some families. They didn't say any names, obviously, but the only thing I can think of is the cop and his nutcase wife that I reported.

Then they started beating me.

For the next five minutes or so, they were kicking me in the head and beating down on me with their nightsticks, and continuing to talk crap to me. Finally, they decided they had enough fun and threw me back in their patrol car with the bag still over my head. They took me back to my car and took me back out.

"We're watching you," they said. "Wait a couple of minutes until you take that shit off." And they threw me down on the ground on the other side of my car, where I wouldn't be seen by anybody driving by. Then, a few more parting words – "You fucked over a lot of our families, don't ever do that shit again."

They drove away and I finally took the bag off my head. For a week, I hurt pretty bad. But soon I was going to experience a whole new level of pain. And it wouldn't be physical pain. It would be the pain of my heart breaking in half.

Chapter 16: J Nasty

J Nasty wasn't doing good.

At least, that's what I kept hearing from my friends. Every time
I saw the dude, he seemed fine, but then I kept hearing he
was loopy and out of it when he saw other people. And he was
always trying to borrow money from them too.

It all seemed to add up to him using again.

To begin with, he shouldn't have been having money
problems. He was still getting pills through his own pain clinic
appointments – and he was also still sponsoring other people
(one doctor at a time now, of course, with the new regulations
in place). So he had enough medication to sell to keep paying
off his debts. But if he was still taking the shit, then that would
explain both him being broke and also acting fucked up
around other people.

I kept warning him over and over again that he shouldn't take the pills. I knew this was dangerous territory for him, so I always told him I'd cut him off if I caught him using. I didn't want to be responsible for anything happening to him. He was my bro, and I wanted him to stay well.

But I kept hearing things. We had the same friends and they let me know what they thought was going on. It was frustrating - around me, he was completely normal. Was he okay? Or did he just make sure he was sober when he knew he was going to see me? I couldn't know for sure.

So I tried to pretend everything was okay.

Then one day, he didn't answer his phone. I kept trying to call him all day long. No answer. No call backs from him either, even though I left a bunch of messages. I was worried. Deep down, I knew something was wrong, so I got more and more anxious when I didn't hear from him.

At 11 o'clock that night, I finally went over to his place and knocked on the door. No answer. Now, alarms were ringing in my head. Something was up.

I had the keys to his apartment, so I went in. He was out like a light – and there were pills fucking everywhere in the place. So I had my answer. He was using all right – and I could see for myself just how bad it had gotten.

That was it. In my mind, it was a done deal with me and him.

I had still been getting him into my clinic for appointments - as long as he only saw the one doctor, there wasn't a problem. But that was all over. I cut him off. I had warned him enough times. I hoped this might turn him around. What the hell else could I do? It was too painful to watch.

Meanwhile, I thought I was in love. Like I said, I was 30 now and I thought it was time to think about starting a family.

I had been seeing a lot of Laura, the girl from the vet's office that I had been dating on and off for 8 years, since when I worked at the Puppy Boutique. I finally made up my mind that she was the one and I went out and bought a ring and everything.

That didn't go over so well. She told me she didn't like the ring. It wasn't good enough for her.

You wanna really piss off a guy? When he proposes, say *that* to him. I took the ring back and we didn't break it off completely, but obviously, it wasn't ever going to be the same. I started realizing that I was a lucky guy – lucky that she hadn't said "Yes."

I was with her a few days after the ring disaster, when I got a call from a friend. He was with his girl and a friend of theirs named Crystal. I had met Crystal a couple of times, but, since I thought I was serious with Laura, I didn't really pursue anything, even though I loved her look. Now my friend was telling me to come over and meet up with him and his girl and Crystal.

"Yo, we're going out," he said. "Crystal's actually asking about you. She knows you're engaged, but I told her that you're not happy. What's going on?"

What was going on? Nothing with Miss Not Good Enough, that was for sure. So I told Laura I was stepping out for a couple of minutes - only it turned out to be a lot longer.

Like forever.

I turned off my phone so Laura wouldn't be able to get in touch with me, then I met my friends and Crystal at a bar with a pool table. We had an amazing time, shooting pool, getting drunk, having fun. Crystal and I went home together and, from that night forward, we talked every day. We just hit it off. She had a good day job. I admired that and was happy to finally find a woman my age that had a job, took care of her responsibilities, and didn't have to run back to Mommy for help. She was on her own and I respected her for it.

I began to feel like she was the one.

But it wasn't smooth sailing. Not by a longshot. I had lived a certain way all my adult life and it was hard to change that. Not that I didn't try. I moved in with Crystal for a while at her place in Fort Lauderdale to try to make a go of it. But we kept having issues, mostly because it was hard for me to really settle down.

The fighting didn't stop. Finally, I couldn't take it anymore and neither could she. I moved out and went back to my place in Sunny Isles. I missed her, but I was too angry to go back. We were both determined not to give in to the other. Before I knew it, three weeks had gone by without us talking.

It was a Sunday morning and I had come home at around 5, drunk and completely wasted. I fell asleep. A few hours later, around noon, still hung over, I got up and took the car out to go get something to eat.

As I was driving, the phone rang. A friend called.

J Nasty was dead.

Oh shit. Shit, shit, shit.

I had to pull over to the side of the street because I was flooded with tears - I couldn't see where I was going. I didn't even know for sure if this was for real – that J Nasty was actually gone. I didn't want it to be true, but I had been so scared of it happening for so long, I couldn't keep down the emotions. It hit me hard, harder than anything else in my life up until that moment. I was screaming and crying and the only thing I could think of to do was to call my mom to tell her. She was a good friend of J Nasty and his family.

It had only been a couple months since I had cut off J Nasty. Since then, I would still get a call from him once in a while, but now he always sounded drugged up. I guess, since I wasn't letting him get pills at the clinic, he felt like he had no reason to pretend in front of me anymore. He'd just laugh at me if I tried to tell him he needed to stop taking that shit. So I'd hang up the phone fast, because it was too hard to talk to him.

I didn't want to hear him like that. I could tell he was falling apart, but, at the same time, it was pretty fucking obvious he wasn't going to do anything to turn himself around. It was horrible. And the most horrible thing about it was that the pills killed him -- the pills I had helped him get and the pills he continued to get on his own.

Anyway, I got it confirmed. The news was on the level -- J was gone. I had to go see him one last time.

J Nasty was living at that time with his sister in Ocala, northwest of Orlando, about 300 miles away. I packed my bags and asked my mom to come with me, since I was in a bad way and didn't want to drive that far without some support. The two of us got there about four hours later and went directly to where he had passed away. I went through his stuff with his sister and my mom and I found his driver's license. I actually kept it and some other small things of his I found.

Then I went with the family to the funeral home. For the first time, I sat through the planning of a funeral. It felt beyond harsh for them to have to make decision after decision about what to do with the body, what kind of service to have, bla bla bla, when none of them could think straight because they were overwhelmed with grief. I tried to do my part by paying for two urns. His sister and me split his ashes, half in one urn, half in the other.

Between the planning and the actual funeral, I had to drive back home with my mom because there was some clinic stuff I had to take care of – and I also needed some decent clothes for the funeral. I got back, reported in to work and told them I was taking a few days off, then I grabbed my suit and some other stuff and headed back to Ocala with a bunch of my buddies who knew J too. They took turns driving my car, while I sat in the back, smoking and drinking the whole way, trying to kill the pain and not succeeding.

But one good thing did happen on that drive back. Crystal had heard about J Nasty's passing away and knew it would've shaken me to my core. Even though we hadn't talked in weeks, she gave me a call to see how I was doing. She said she was sad that I hadn't called her when I got the bad news, because she wished she could have gone with me and be there for me. Then she told me we had to get together after the funeral, we had to talk. I said, yeah, sure.

I missed her. No doubt she could have helped me get through this better.

The sad thing is I ended up missing most of the funeral. There were a couple of people in J Nasty's life that I knew had helped mess him up – to be specific, a girl who was two-timing him and a fellow junkie that would encourage him to use too much. I felt both of them had hurt J and never really cared what happened to him. When they showed up for the service, I bit my tongue for the sake of J Nasty's family, but I just couldn't be in the same room with them for long. During the funeral, I stood out in the parking lot most of the time. I couldn't deal with those people – or maybe I couldn't deal with the fact that J Nasty was really gone.

Who really killed J Nasty? Maybe you could blame those two sleazeballs. Maybe you could blame J for not looking out for himself. But that wasn't the whole story. When it came to all the victims of the insane pill mill years, the culprits included the State of Florida, the pill companies, all the greedy clinic owners and doctors, not to mention lower-level operators like me (even though I had tried to protect him), who all had made it easy for people like J Nasty to get hooked. This was the result of all the corruption and moneygrubbing, the result of everybody lining their pockets without a thought about the damage that could be done by letting millions of pills flood the street -- a dead kid that deserved better.

I made a vow that day. I was done with doing my dirty work.

I had already stopped most of my sponsoring because of the prescription tracking, but I was still helping a couple people get pills from our doctors at that point – all clean and legally. But J Nasty's death was the end of it for me. I just stopped. I couldn't be a part of this madness anymore. I had always told myself that the pill-poppers were adults who could make their own decisions – that made it okay in my mind for me to do what I did.   But it wasn't okay anymore.

It couldn't be when my best friend was no longer breathing.

My friends and I left Ocala and drove back to South Florida drunk and silly and stupid. When I got home, I went over to Crystal's. She got out of work early to see me, because she said she has some news for me.

She was pregnant – with my child.

This was crazy. Really crazy. The Lord had taken someone out of my life that I loved – and suddenly, brought somebody new into it at the exact same time. Even though I was going through one of the hardest things I would ever face in my life, I felt a wave of joy at Crystal's news. Maybe God knew I did what I could for J. Maybe He knew I was really sincere about changing up my life.

My beautiful daughter Nadia is two years old as I write these words. And I'm a very proud daddy – not to mention a happy husband.

Yeah, Crystal thought the ring I got her was good enough.

Chapter 17: Endgame

You couldn't escape the headlines.

The clean-up from the pill mill party was in full swing. And the ones who had partied the hardest were now in the deepest shit.

The infamous George twins had their four clinics – or maybe I should say, ATMs - shut down by the Feds. Agents moved in and took away everything they had made from their practices, including a few six-bedroom houses, a shopping plaza, four-figure Rolex and Patek Phillippe watches, luxury boats, and fast and expensive cars like their Lamborghini Murcielago - not to mention the over 3 million bucks left in their bank accounts. Even then, there were tens of millions of dollars the authorities never did track down. "They were swimming in money. Obscene," one Fed told the *Fort Lauderdale Sun-*

Sentinel. Yeah, but the real obscenity was the 56 drug overdose deaths that were tracked back to their clinics.

Then "Pill Mill Vinny" went down. The Feds took $12 million in cash, cars, boats and property off of him. Again, there was a lot they didn't get – the DEA estimated he made at least $22 million between 2008 and 2011 (which, I guess, explained why he didn't sweat 200 grand sitting out on his desk while he did business). Vinny did a plea bargain and copped to drug, money-laundering and income tax crimes – but was still looking at maybe 20 years in jail. But that wasn't going to be a new experience for him - he had already done time for heroin and cocaine dealing before he opened his clinics. How did a convicted drug dealer get to run medical practices in the first place? I don't know, ask the State of Florida.

It was suddenly so bad that even Roberto's clinic got in trouble.

He was still running the place Isaac had set up for him. But Isaac got caught with his pants down when the state kept making tougher and tougher regulations. Isaac didn't know he needed to get a new kind of license to stay in business until it was too late – and when he did finally find out, he didn't have enough time to get it approved. The DEA was watching them closely for whatever reason, so, when Isaac didn't get the paperwork in by the deadline, they instantly swooped in and shut down the office. Isaac got arrested, but, since Roberto was just an employee, he walked free and clear.

But suddenly, Roberto didn't have a job. So he called me and told me what went down, wondering if I could get him back in at my place. I went to Gabe about him, figuring I'd get turned down. But, to my surprise, Gabe said, "Yeah, we'll hire him back."

Turns out what Gabe *really* wanted was Roberto's list of patients from his old clinic. Over the next three months, Roberto contacted them all and tried to get as many as he could to make appointments with us. And once Roberto did all that, once Gabe had gotten everything he could out of him, Gabe turned around and fired him.

What a sweetheart.

I was pissed, but what could I do? Luckily, Roberto finally ended up with a new job – as a sales rep for a pharmaceutical company. Stick with what you know, as they say.

And speaking of sticking with what you know, I was working on my own exit plan based on my unique skill set. As I said, weed had become legal in Washington State in 2012. Gabe was always talking to me about it and I thought maybe I could move to Seattle and start growing again. I wouldn't have to worry about hurricanes, landlords or the power company – once I was licensed, I could do it right out in the open, legally. I had saved a pile of money from all my hustling and was ready to make the move.

Problem was, I couldn't get anybody in Seattle to rent me a house long distance. And I knew if I flew up there and showed my tattooed self in person, they would *definitely* turn me down. I had a partner up there I was working with, so I said to him, "Dude, why don't you rent the house? I'll wire the money to your account once you get it, just put it in your name and we'll work it out. We'll get our licenses, you'll live there or I will when I get there. We'll figure something out." But he was in his own little world and not really motivated to help me get started. Without that connection, I was stuck. I didn't want to move out there and blow all my money on something that might not work out.

I still had my heart set on it, though and Gabe kept acting really interested in my new potential career path. He always wanted to talk about me growing in Seattle. Was this what I really wanted to do? Would I be happy doing it? Yeah and yeah were my answers. Well, he would say, when you get out there, you could maybe help us get our marijuana tracking technology sold out there, the technology that could track weed from seed to sale and catch any stolen pot. Sure, I'd say, it sounded like an awesome idea. He acted like we were gonna be partners.

It was late 2012 and Kevin Grossman, the guy who helped me throw out the cop and his wife, was still Gabe and Pete's CEO of the year. He was a nice guy, in his 50's maybe, a great human being and I really liked him. And he would talk honestly about the problems he was having working for Gabe and Pete. They treated him like shit like they treated everybody like shit. They talked down to him and made him do all kinds of crap he shouldn't have had to involve himself in.

Here's something I need to explain so you understand what happened next. If you're running a Florida corporation, you have to file what they call an Annual Report, where you state the address of your business and who's running it. The state lets you do this online every year at their SunBiz.Org site, and it's easy enough, not much to it beyond what I just told you.

Well, one day, Gabe and Pete had Kevin double-check something on the site – and he noticed something really weird. And I mean REALLY fucking weird.

I was listed as *the President of the whole company.*

Oh yeah, and, apparently, I was the Treasurer too. And I had some other title that started with the letter "D," but neither of us could figure out what that was all about. Whatever, my name was all over this thing – but Gabe and Pete's names were nowhere to be seen. In Florida's eyes, I was the guy *solely responsible* for the whole fucking place.

WTF???????

Now, I never agreed to any of this – and I didn't sign any paperwork authorizing them to use my name like this.
So...what the hell did they do this for? Then I remembered what happened with Roberto when his clinic got busted. Isaac, the guy running the clinic, went to jail – and the employee, Roberto, got off scot-free.

Holy fuck. I was the guy running the clinics, according to the official records. They made *me* out to be Isaac.

It made sense. Gabe and Pete must have been close to pissing their pants with pill mills going down left and right in Broward County. Even though they had tried to keep their clinics looking as legit as possible, they still must've panicked and figured if they put my name down as the head honcho, they'd get out of any legal liability if the Feds came knocking.

This was too much. Kevin didn't want me to say anything to the Dynamic Duo, but how could I just forget about something like this? I had a kid now – and I was engaged to Crystal. I didn't want my life fucked up by those two freaks. I had to do something.

But it turned out I didn't have to. I don't know if Kevin told them I knew or what, but, after a few days, Gabe came to me with the paperwork I needed to sign to get my name taken off the company's Annual Report. Naturally I asked, "Hey - how did my name get on there as President?" He stumbled around, trying to make up some kind of explanation, but the fact was he didn't have a good answer.

The only answer was a real fucking bad one.

I took all the papers home and studied them. I finally signed them and then followed up to make sure my name got removed from the official company listing. That's when things really started to go south with Gabe and Pete. Turned out that was the only thing they were keeping me around for – to be the patsy who went to jail in their place.

Like Roberto, I had outlived my usefulness. To begin with, in their eyes, I had become too expensive. As I said, I was making around 60k by then and they knew they could get somebody for a lot cheaper – somebody who didn't have to be covered in tattoos. Since the patients weren't crazy junkies anymore, Gabe and Pete didn't need my street skills to run the place. They could just hire a straight-up by-the-book person to manage the clinic.

So Gabe stepped up the talk about me moving to Seattle – pushing me to go ahead and do it, making it sound like it would be the best thing for me and that he would help me once I got there. He also stepped up the pressure on me, complaining that I needed to get more patients into the clinic, to make them more money, because the old flood of patients had dried up to a trickle.

I couldn't change the fact that times had changed and it wasn't the Wild West anymore. The game was over. There was nothing more that could be done. That was the truth – and Gabe and Pete knew it. This was just about pushing me out the door.

Gabe stopped dealing with me directly - he'd send Kevin to talk to me instead, and Kevin would have to tell me the exact same shit about how I should get more patients in for appointments. He knew as well as I did that there was no miracle cure to turn things around, but he had to do his job.

Then they brought in a new Medical Assistant for me to train.

This guy was in his mid-twenties and, even though his last gig was as a bartender, he still had more legitimate medical experience than me – for example, he could draw blood, which I never did. The idea was he would do all the medical prep for the patients and I would focus on keeping the records in order, so we stayed good with the DEA and the Department of Health. Okay, fine. But then this kid started studying the filing system and seemed real interested in how that end of the business worked, even though that supposedly wasn't in his job description. And he learned it quick. It wasn't that hard.

Well, after a few weeks, after he had everything figured out, this kid comes to me bitching that Gabe isn't paying him enough. And that he's going on a job interview to get out of there. Okay, fine, whatever.

The following Monday, July 22nd, 2013, I came in to work as usual – but the kid's not there. I figure he must have gotten that other job, but, Jesus, it would have been nice to let me know.

But then again, something seems fishy.

His stethoscope and a couple other things of his were still in the office. Wouldn't he need all that if he was starting another job? Why wouldn't he have taken his stuff? And why didn't he call and tell me he wasn't coming in?

An hour and a half goes by. Suddenly, Gabe shows up. And, with his head down, he pulls me into a back office.

Then I immediately know what's going down.

Gabe sits down and says, "You know where this is going."

I play dumb and I answer, "No, I don't know where this is going, where's it going?"

He tells me about how he knows I'm not happy there and this and that. Bullshit, of course. I tell him about how I thought I was going to go to Washington and grow and help get his hi-tech tracking shit sold.

He says, "No, this is where we have to part ways."

"Part ways?" I say. "I thought we were friends and we were gonna keep doing business together."

"Well," he says, being careful with his words, "We are real friends, but…I think I'm doing you a favor. You really want to go grow, so now you can."

In my mind, I'm jumping across the table, beating the shit out of him. I'm watching his fat face get smashed in with my fists. I'm releasing 9 years of anger at how he treated me, treated

Roberto, treated everybody who worked for him and Pete so they could waste as much money as humanly possible on as much stupid overpriced crap as possible. I'm pounding and pounding him over and over, until his designer suit is caked with blood.

But I have to make all that go away. I have to remember, I got a kid. I got a woman I love. I gotta keep my job for now.

So I bargain. I'm getting a salary for an 8 hour day, but, at this point, we're only open around 5 hours a day, because there aren't enough patients to keep us fulltime. So let's remove that problem. I offer to go on hourly pay, and just make the money for those 5 hours. I'll be part-time. Seems to me that makes sense. Why wouldn't Gabe take that deal?

"No, no," he says, "We've got to part ways. When I come in here and watch you on the cameras, it doesn't look like your head's in the game anymore."

Really? I run your shit, all that goes on here, and I make you millions by keeping everything running smooth. Everything. I lie for you; I bend over backwards to get patients. I do all this different shit for you, but now it's like that? It's just get the fuck out of here?

I kept it together, but it was hard. My "exit interview" was finally over after a couple more awkward minutes. When I went back out in the lobby, there was a girl sitting there, ready to interview for the MA position.

That was the last piece of the puzzle – now I saw how I had been set up. The kid who I trained was going to run the place instead of me - and this chick was going to be the new MA. The whole thing was a scam, the kid was in on it, there was no job interview and he didn't show that day because he knew they were going to can me. And he didn't want to be there in case I felt like kicking his ass all over the place until he needed some real pain management.

I packed up my stuff. I had felt this coming for a few weeks, so I had already taken a few things home, some baby pictures and what not, but this was definitely the end of the road. While

I packed up a box with the rest of my things, they had somebody standing by me, watching what I was taking, to make sure I don't do anything crazy.

And to think just a few months before this, I had owned the place!

But now, it was over. I left and never looked back.

To tell you the truth, I was relieved.

The funny thing is, you stomp out one fire and another one starts burning. Even though Florida cleaned up the Oxy problem, now there are new headlines popping up about more people using heroin around here. I guess if somebody needs a fix, they're gonna find it somewhere. That was J Nasty's problem. You can't save somebody who doesn't want to save themselves. But I still miss the guy.

In the meantime, Broward County has found a new way to profit off this shit – in 2012, addiction treatment centers here saw an 87 percent jump in business from heroin addicts. I guess it's progress that they're treating it instead of enabling it.

As for me, I miss living the high life. It was nice going to a mall and not having to worry about what you spent, because you knew, the next week, you were going to earn big again. Luckily I put away what I did earn, but that's not gonna last forever.

The fact is, the American Dream is a little out of reach for guys like me these days. That's why I did what I did – it was the only way I saw myself earning a decent living. I managed to grab on to a higher rung on the ladder for a few years, but I couldn't keep my grip – because, it turned out, that ladder wasn't real in the first place.

But I'm hanging in there. Colorado legalized pot too, and now a lot of other states, including Florida, are thinking about doing the same. I'll be growing again soon and I won't have to look over my shoulder when I do it this time around. And I'll be smarter with my money this time around too.

And I guess that's the real upside to this whole crazy story. I'm older, I'm wiser, and fuck it, I'm still here. I was pushed to my limits and kept my cool. And along the way, I ran a multi-million dollar business – and did a pretty fucking amazing job of it. Me, the guy with no college degree.

So I'm ready for the next phase of my life and my next adventure, and I have two amazing people to share it with – my wife and my daughter. Which is why I got just one last tattoo to get.

It's gonna be the date I married Crystal.

About the Authors

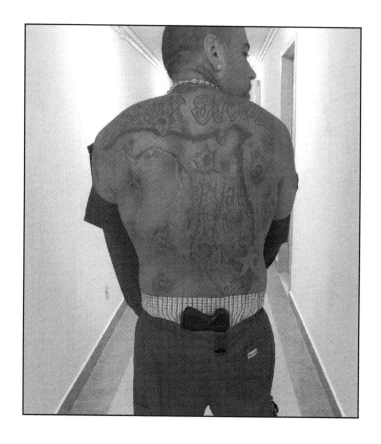

Christian Valdes is a Cuban-American who, from 2004 to 2013, managed several infamous "pill mills" in South Florida and ran his own secret pill operation right under his bosses' noses for 5 of those years. He currently resides in Sunny

Isles, in the North Miami area of Florida, with his wife and daughter.

Joel and Lisa Canfield are New York-based ghostwriters who have worked on many best-selling book projects involving notable business and entertainment figures. Their most recent book, *What's Driving You???: How I Overcame Abuse and Learned to Lead in the NBA*, the autobiography of NBA veteran Keyon Dooling, was released in July of 2014.

In loving memory. Rest in peace: J Nasty.

Made in the USA
Middletown, DE
04 December 2016